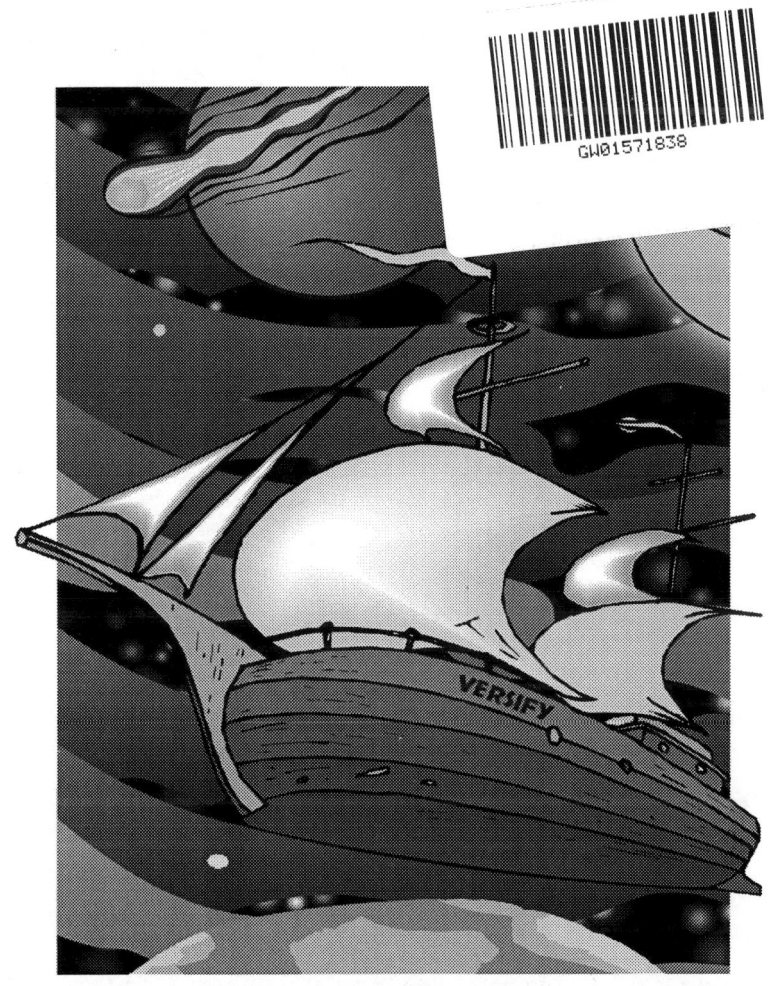

POETIC VOYAGES
BRISTOL VOL I

Edited by Simon Harwin

First published in Great Britain in 2002 by
YOUNG WRITERS
Remus House,
Coltsfoot Drive,
Peterborough, PE2 9JX
Telephone (01733) 890066

All Rights Reserved

Copyright Contributors 2001

HB ISBN 0 75433 418 X
SB ISBN 0 75433 419 8

FOREWORD

Young Writers was established in 1991 with the aim to promote creative writing in children, to make reading and writing poetry fun.

This year once again, proved to be a tremendous success with over 88,000 entries received nationwide.

The Poetic Voyages competition has shown us the high standard of work and effort that children are capable of today. It is a reflection of the teaching skills in schools, the enthusiasm and creativity they have injected into their pupils shines clearly within this anthology.

The task of selecting poems was therefore a difficult one but nevertheless, an enjoyable experience. We hope you are as pleased with the final selection in *Poetic Voyages Bristol Vol 1* as we are.

CONTENTS

Cherry Garden Primary School
David Godfrey	1
Laura Filer	1
Lucy Rees	2
George Griffiths	2
Chelsea Perry	3
Ashley Gould	3
Jordan Smith	4
Tom Hodgkinson	4
Luke Denham	5
Matthew Lord	6
Kerry Summerhayes	6
Ben Williamson	7
Jennifer Dick	8
Jack Chubbuck	8
Matthew Swanborough	9
William Footitt	10
Jay Cunningham	10
Avril Davis	11
Darryll Bennett	11
Kayleigh Parsons	12
Roxanna Vennard	13
Amy Farrant	14
Jude Smith	14
Harry Webb	15

Colston's Collegiate Lower School
Marcella Pinto	16
Esther Carter	16
Helena Stott	17
Jaime Bracewell	18
Alice Jess Carpenter	18
Emily Ebers	19
Sophie Baber	20
David John Fiander Stone	21
Stephanie Lewis	22

Claire Whyard	22
Rowan Winstone	23
Mark Edward Roberts	24
Alexander Beaves	24
Aimée Marshall	25
Ross Martinovic	25
Abigail Nicole Litten	26
Kit Sheppard	26
Eric Underwood	27
Amelia Beaton	28
George Lloyd	28
Charles Hill	29
Annabel Paterson	29
Thomas C A Fisher	30
Peter Wollaston	30
Emma-Claire Reed	31
William Brown	32
Daniel Watchurst	32
Rachael Moss	33
Jack Harris	34
Julian Walcott-gordon	34
Jamie FitzHenry	35
Michael O'Reilly	35
Sarah Vincent	36
Matthew Narey	36
Ashley Maggs	37
Christopher Maggs	37
Harriet Campbell	38
Shaun Malone	38
Thomas Jelley	39
George Tucker	40
David Jackson	40
Jordan Underhill	41
Jayne Hulin	41
Alex Underhill	42
Max Tarr	42
Edward Philip	43
James Laver	43

Amy Lowndes	44
Samuel Ford	44
Harbhajan Singh Baryah	45
Aaron Sealey Grant	45
Aaron Farrel	46
Duncan Lambert	46
Simon Charles Gilbert	47
David Cruickshank	47
Tom Harris	48
Maddy Thomas	48
Katie Mason	49
Ashleigh Elizabeth Wayne	49
Kyp Bridgen	50
Jay Drew	50
Stuart Bannerman	51
Jonathan Pickup	51
Aaron Burrell	52
Miriam Mathieson	52
Andrew Croxson	53
Jonathan Mason	53
Jenny Jones	54
Andrew Beaves	54
Rebecca Whitehead	55
Max Semple	56
Peter Davies	57
William Olpin	57
Ben Krawiec	58
Samuel Gardiner	58
Ben Deeley	59

Filton Avenue Junior School

Charlotte Alleyne	60
Hannah Richards	60
Adrian Price	60

Henleaze Junior School

Connor Smith	61
Laura Sudworth	62

Zoe Jeffery	62
Charlotte Husher	63
George E Day	64
Eleanor Head	64
Jared Stride	65
Matt Jones	65
Abigail Smith	66
Simon Foale	66
Sophie Buchanan	67
Claire Sangster	67
Robbie White	68
Carla Ahmadi	68
Benedict Campbell	69
Katie Andrews	69
Saskia Daller	70
Sophie Mason	70
Catharine Hiley	71
Caitlin Barnbrook	71
Melissa Catalano	72
Emily Thompson	72
David Wilkinson	73
Christian George	73
Charlotte Russell-Smith	74
Henry Phillips	74
Jennifer Brierley	75
Adel Chowdhury	75
Elena Deakin	76
Sophie Fletcher	76
Sophie Stephens	77
Hannah Cooper	78
Jenny Croker	78
Louise Jones	79
Katie White	79
Richard Foale	80
Rebecca Heryet	81
Harriet Buckner	82
William Rowe	83
William Jenkinson	84

Rebecca Shuttleworth	85
Jessica Ardis	85
Jenny Nicholls	86
Emily White	86
Mahdi Shariff	87
Polly Northam	87
Isabelle White	88
Jonathan Appleby	88
Rosalind McClelland	89
Philippa Campbell	89
Josephine Holloway	90
Lucy Catherine Rowe	90
Hannah Levene	91
Kelcy Harvey	91
Hannah Lewis	92
Gene Jozefowicz	92
Jack Radford-Sidney	93
Rosamund Thomas	93
Matt Quaife	94
Helen White	94
Anna Barham	95
David Cutler	95
Jonathan Maszuchin	96
David James Benjamin Clark	97
Matthew McCoubrey	98
Kyana Wambui Gitahi	98
Emily Reeves	99
Nicola Rees	99
Sophie Helena Moody	100
Edward Benjamin	100
Charlotte Seymour	101
Tamar Nunn	101
Amy Willerton	102
Emily Greenslade	102
Andrew Watts	103
Lauren Davies	103
Lucy Gilbert	104
Robert Newman	104

Sophia Kallias	105
Zoe Bond	105
Hilary Orchard	106
Isobel Booth	106
Tara-Louise Seddon	107
David Cook	107
Hope Gallie	108
Daniel Kohn	108
Aseel Basson	109
Alanna Hyde	109
Emily Adcock	110
Catherine Holloway	110
Emily Daly	111
Harriet Booth	112
Michael Cook	112
Vicki Jane Squires	113
David Mark Cordell	113
Luke Steven	114
Niall Spencer	114

Hillcrest Primary School

Joshua Greenfield	115
Rory McLoughlin	115
Josie Berry	116
Jethro Gilbert	116
Jacob Lamb	117
Sally Langdon	118
Anna Milby	118
Alice Wyatt	119
Ellena Caudwell	119
Dorothy Thompson	120
Ruby Bell	120
Emily Burke	121
Alex Youé	121
Rebecca Harvey	122
Emily Nicholas	123
Lucy Stephens	124
Harry Byrne	124

Anna Barlow	125
Jess Roome	126
Elizabeth Studley	126
Joseph Bowles	127
Theo Bond	127
Omar Ali	128
Alex Rose	128
Caroline Sinclair	129

Longwell Green Primary School

Zoe Brock	129
Katie Manfield	130
Christopher Miller	130
Abigail McCarthy	131
Richard James & Mike Cox	131
Becky Garland	132
Leah Saunders & Charlotte Smith	132
Stephanie Youmans	133
Ryan Cleaves	133
Rebecca Dimes	134
James Clover	134
Jenny Selman	134
Rachel Seel	135
Claire Uppington	135
Hayley Benjamin	135
Michael Stinson	136
Andrew Selman	136
Beth Doyle	137
Daniel Whybrew	137
Sophie Worsfold	138
David Cardy	138
Michael Thomas	139
Becki Keen	139
Georgina Dann	140
Joshua Willis	140
Emma Youmans	140
Simon Lewis	141
Lewis Toghill	141

James Dix	141
Lucy Davis	142
Alice Drury Webb	142
Liam Jacques	142
Jack Denning	143
Alex Ash	143
Leanne Pople	143
Grace Lewis	144
Edward Downing	144
Emma Alway	145
Josie Smith	145
Stephanie Cox	146
Lauren Mitchell	146
Andrew Smith	147
Chelsie Galdies	147
Abigail Allen	148
Bradley Cox	148
Claire Moon	149
Tommy Cains	149
Sophie Bignell	150
Samuel Bray	150
Chloé Nowell	151
Matthew Oliver	152
Stephen Walter	152
April Oxenham	153
Thomas Francis	154
Rebecca Dale	154
Alex Hayes	155
Melanie Williamson	156
Alex Martin	156
Louise Hendy	157
Tom Churches	158
Joe Stansfield	158

Luckwell Primary School

Claire Case	158
Marcus Guldbert-Allen	159
Lewis Gilbert	159

Ben Collett	160
Michael Bawn	160
Kerry Coles	161
Charlotte Overy	161
Matthew Hellier	162
Katie Burge	162
George Cox	163
Sophie Jenkins	163
Dale Bright	164
Jordan Marsh	164
Paul Rhodes	165
Lauren Stone	165
Chelsea Emma Harris	166
Katie Townsend	166
Lauren Fay Stuckes	167
George Tom Smith	167
James Trenchard	168
Amy March	168
Jemma Hicks	169
Elliot Smith	169
Hannah Milkins	170
Oliver Chalkley-Brown	170
Tom Delaney	171
Jorja Jones	171
Amy Smith	172
Shauna Charles	172
Rachel Moore	173
Gemma Woodburn	173
Eloise Heybyrne	174
Michael Thomas	174
Kelly Anne Booth	175
Adam Beasmore	175
Rachel Jones	176
Frankie Marks	176
Martin Chamberlain	177
Iona Baker	177
Charlotte Stoddart	178
Thomas Wilkox	178

Tim Jones	178
Luke Kibby	179
Rory Notton	179
Danielle Upham	179
Charlotte Daw	180
Dan Howard	180
Conner Glanville	181
Thomas Reading	181
Callum Herbert	182
Blaine Carroll	182
Alex Mallett	183
May Barnes	183
Chelsea Tanner	184
Ryan Stuckes	184
Laura Rhodes	185
George Nelmes	185
Giorgio Mancini	186
Tayler Maggs	187
Sophie Christopher	187
James Powell	188
James Charles	188
Sam Skidmore	189
Tom Hill	189
Ricky Barrett	190
Joe Care	190
Mathew Wherlock	191
Benito Mancini	191

Oldbury Court Primary School

Rebecca Weaver	192
Sam Fletcher	192
Elly Robbins	193
Eliot Glasspole	193
Courtenay Grey	194
Jade Phillips	195
Levi Mapstone	195
Sophie Jane Brine	196

Shirehampton Primary School
Ceejay Dun & Alex West	196
Amberley Gazzard	197
Charlotte Allan & Dannielle Harris	197
Christopher James Higgs	197
Amy Hembrough & Jordhanna Hudson	198
Jessica Lenagh	198
Kelsey Cox & Kimberley Sheppard	199
Luke Daniel Krupa	199
Amy Richardson	200

SS Peter & Paul RC Primary School
Teresa Licata	200
Davide Lattuca	201
Daniella Ruffino	201
Simon White	202
Tom Wright	202
Johnny Creamer	203
Sophie O'Kelly	203
David McCalley	204
Kei Bergh	204
Lauren Cherry	205
Louise Marie Celine Walker	206
Callum Craig	206
Jakita Anderson	207
Simone Price	208
Sean Rice	208
Mahanagh Adams	209
Phoebe Farrell	209
Cian O'Carroll-Lolait	210
Kasia Everett	211
Roisin Walsh	212
Anthony Brandrick	212
Tyrone Shaw	213
Cecile Jones	213
Aishu Subramanyain	214
Phoebe Potter	214
Jamie Connett	215

	Emily Poole	215
	Angelo Amato	216
	Amelia Scanlan	216
	Remi Bergh	216
	Katie Creamer	217
	Sean O'Kelly	217
	William Foster-Grundy	218
	Perran Mitchell	218
	Hannah Giebus	219
	Hope Alkins	219
	Claudia Gocoul	219
	Lydia Kellett	220
	Eleanor King	220
The Tynings School		
	Connie Short	221
	Kate-Louise Fry	221
	Claudia Jacob	222
	Faye Anastasia Mason	222
	Jack Andrews	223
	Samantha Wood	223
	Jordan Powell	224
	Sophie Graham	224

The Poems

WHAT IS YELLOW?

Yellow is the colour of a rubber duck,
And sunflower petals,
And my homework book.
It's the sun and a lemon,
And a banana,
It's a whipped up egg yolk
And a warm feeling,
Butter, custard
Both are yellow.
Beams of a torch
And my sister's locks,
So are workman's coats,
And a summer's day.
A bright look on some
And cheese in a bun,
Sweetcorn and buttercups,
And good news.

David Godfrey (11)
Cherry Garden Primary School

WHAT IS RED?

Red is the colour of blood,
And wine
From red grapes
Ripened in the crimson sun.
Red is the colour of a rose,
The reflection of my undying love,
As seen from my burning heart.

Laura Filer (10)
Cherry Garden Primary School

WHAT IS YELLOW?

Yellow is the colour of a burning sun
And the colour of a buttered bun.
The colour of an old man's teeth
And custard, good to eat.
A yellow sweet.
The colour of a singing canary bird.
A big yellow firework, from far away heard.
The colour of a daffodil
And more still.
A homework book, nearly full,
Spaghetti, sweetcorn,
Piled up tall.
The fingers of a bad smoker
And honey on the legs of a bee.

Lucy Rees (10)
Cherry Garden Primary School

WHAT IS GREEN?

Green is a Christmas tree
In a forest
Ready to be cut down
Green is a Christmas tree
In my living room
With green lights that shine
And light up the whole room
Baubles of green on my Christmas tree
And tinsel sparkling like glitter
To make another forest of green.

George Griffiths (11)
Cherry Garden Primary School

PLANET GOOGLE

This musty place, I come across
Dead
Dusty and dry
Green with black spots
Sleek and smooth
Inhumane
Unspirited.
Nothing disturbs this planet
Unheard of.
No wind
No rain
No sea
A place I wouldn't like to be.

Chelsea Perry (10)
Cherry Garden Primary School

WHAT IS WHITE?

White is the colour of a winter sky
When the colour of winter drops
White is the colour of a smoky cloud
And the colour of Miss' white board
It's the colour of wadding
Inside a slipper
And the colour of the pages in our book
And white walls in my hallway
The colour of the card
I got sent today
White erases black pen
When I go wrong

Ashley Gould (10)
Cherry Garden Primary School

WHAT IS RED?

Red is the colour of Santa's hat
And a ladybird's back
And Rudolph's nose glowing brightly.
Red is the colour of a poppy in the sun
And a rich red rose.
Red is the colour of blushed cheeks
And a postbox in the road.
Beaming down the street, fire engines
They're red too.
A crab is red, crawling in the rock pools
And the sunset that creeps to the sky.
Red is the colour of someone's heart
That is beating and beating.
Christmas stockings are red
Full of toys for Christmas Day.
Red is the colour of bubblegum.
Red leaves on a tree that get hold of
Me.

Jordan Smith (10)
Cherry Garden Primary School

WHAT IS RED?

Red is the colour of blood
And an *angry* bull's eyes,
And a raging fire.

It's autumn leaves and scented roses
And a fire extinguisher,
It's danger
And a strawberry slush-puppie.

It's Boudicca's hair
And our school colour.
Red is also *Santa's* suit
And *Rudolph's* nose.

All of these
Are
Red.

Tom Hodgkinson (11)
Cherry Garden Primary School

THE RINGS OF SATURN

I orbit the rings of Saturn
Freely.
I view the light orange atmosphere,
The scenery,
I see sharp, rusty rocks,
Spitting,
Spitting out,
Deadly,
Vicious,
Red fireballs.
The fireballs stay in mid-air
Floating because of gravity.
As I feel the deadliness of
Fear
As I pass the forbidden rings of
Hell.
The molten *lava* scalds and
Kills.

Luke Denham (10)
Cherry Garden Primary School

WHAT IS RED?

Red is the colour of danger.
Red is fear.
Red is a fire engine,
And blood is red.
A blazing fire,
A car,
An old telephone box,
A postbox,
And a London bus.
Red is beetroot, tomato and pepper,
Apples, strawberries and raspberries too.
Red is Christmas
With Rudolph's red nose
And Father Christmas' cloak and red hat.
Holly berries,
Red baubles,
And candles.

Matthew Lord (10)
Cherry Garden Primary School

WHAT IS RED?

Red is the sound of a trumpet,
Like a deep shade of fire.
Red is like the petals of a rose,
Blowing in the wind.

Red is blood gushing from your veins,
And red a warning sign,
Warning you to go quick if you don't want to get hurt.
Red is a burn that stings like a bee.

Red is when you're angry,
Like you've never been before.
Red is a celebrity's carpet,
That rolls along the floor.

Kerry Summerhayes (10)
Cherry Garden Primary School

WHAT IS RED?

Red is the colour of Father Christmas
And Rudolph's nose glowing in the night
And my school reading folder.
It's a rosy colour
But a danger colour too
And can be a very fine paint.
It's a fire colour.
Chewing gum can be red
So can a brick,
A flowerpot and some rock-solid wood.
A strawberry,
A cherry
All of them are red.
A robin's chest too.
When you dream
You can dream about red.
A beetroot can be red sometimes.
My school jumper is.
It can be a book.
You can get red wine.
My dad is pleased.
Red is the best colour.

Ben Williamson (10)
Cherry Garden Primary School

WHAT IS WHITE?

White is the colour of a bride's wedding dress
And the snow
And Santa's beard
And clouds of cotton wool.
White is the colour of icebergs
And polar bears
And moonlit nights.
It's the colour of a new slipper sole
And the skin of a drum
And sticky dough.
White is my nan's hair
And my grandad's car.
It's the colour of a freshly-washed shirt
Or a freshly-baked roll.
It's the colour of chewing gum
And the envelope of a card
For Christmas!

Jennifer Dick (10)
Cherry Garden Primary School

WHAT IS WHITE?

White is the colour of freezing snow
And chalk on a board
And paper
Clean and new.

It's the colour of walls
In a Spanish land
And the wool
Of a young lamb.

White is the colour of a brand new rubber
And the top of a Guinness
And clouds
White
Fluffy.

It's polystyrene
And new tissues
A sock when it's been washed.

Jack Chubbuck (11)
Cherry Garden Primary School

THE STABLE I OFFERED

Working hard,
Walking on,
Then I heard a knock,
A knock at the door.
It was a couple,
Mary,
Joseph,
A baby Mary carried.
They asked for a room,
A stable I offered.
They took it.
I was really quite lucky,
A King,
The Son of God,
Was born,
In my stable.

Matthew Swanborough (10)
Cherry Garden Primary School

DEAD MAN'S LAND

I see huge, immense rings,
Dead, dark, dingy,
Small dusty planet,
Rust coloured,
Volcanic explosion,
Making orange light splinters from behind,
Small ashes fly below,
Never touched before,
The atmosphere passed away,
Long gone,
The sky worn out by time,
No meteors have hit,
Not a thing has passed by.
I'd better retreat quick.

William Footitt (10)
Cherry Garden Primary School

WHAT IS RED?

Red is the colour of danger!
And love
And a bleeding dove
Red is the heart of love
Red is the colour of the morning sky
And a filled with blood mosquito fly
Red at night, shepherd's delight
Red is the colour of the devil's fright.

Jay Cunningham (10)
Cherry Garden Primary School

THE TRIP TO SPACE

As I fly above, through the gloomy sky,
Passing all the birds that love to fly,
Ahead I see a glowing light,
Fiery red smoke and sparks so bright,
I'm getting closer by the minute,
Is there life on this strange planet?
We were there at last,
My heart was pounding.
At least we've made a safe grounding.
I see hot and fiery dust on the floor,
I'm rather scared to come out of the door.
My home is on Earth.
Of that I am sure.

Avril Davis (11)
Cherry Garden Primary School

THE RINGS

In my planet of skateboarding
There's loads to play.
Fiery craters in the ground.
There's fiery ramps and there's fire.
The fire is orange and red
And it is hot like the sun.
My place is hot and weightless
The Milky Way is next to my planet.
The volcanic ash on the floor.
At night it sits in the dark.

Darryll Bennett (10)
Cherry Garden Primary School

DONKEY

When I was chosen
I did such a pretty pose.
They picked me,
I was gobsmacked.
Mary, that was her name,
She said I was
The cutest one there.
I was excited,
I had an urge
That this was going to be
A big adventure.
We started walking,
Walking and more walking,
Through the dusty roads
Until we finally go there.
I waited outside the inn
While Mary and Joseph
Went to ask for a room.
When Mary came out
I saw the tears in her eyes.
The innkeeper came back out
And said,
'We have got somewhere
But it will do.'
When we got in
We had such a surprise,
It was a stable.
The innkeeper said,
'That's all we've got!'
Mary said,
'If that's all you have got
I'll take it!'

Kayleigh Parsons (10)
Cherry Garden Primary School

PLANET UNKNOWN

After travelling through the Black Sea,
With broken shards of glass.
We see some flashing.
A fog of blues, purples and greens appear.
'Turn round!' I shouted.
We saw a planet unknown.
Loudly thunder howled,
Bright lightning clawed the planet.
There are red spots like blooming roses,
Lighting up the planet like a light bulb.
We circle closer.
The red spots are desert lands.
The desert sand is tomato-red.
And water as green as grass.
Volcanic action everywhere.
Circle once;
Blues, greens and purple is a freezer,
Dead ice slipping and sliding.
This is not a place to be.
You do not feel like you're in your home.
Circle twice;
Red spots are gardens.
Pretty, red, giant flowers.
Blues are rivers running,
Purples are shaggy old mountains,
Green is everything else.
This is the place to be!
You do feel at home!
All the way home we go,
Through the Black Sea,
With broken shards of glass . . .

Roxanna Vennard (10)
Cherry Garden Primary School

PLANET FUZZ BALL

I see a planet
As I travel into space
It's called the planet
Fuzz Ball
It is yellow and fuzzy
I watch it bouncing
Through the air
As I land the ship
It is soft, fluffy and feathery
In its atmosphere
With powder puff treetops
And candyfloss mountains
With fuzzy balls jumping about
All this is undisturbed
So I take-off
Leaving the untouched land
To grow

Amy Farrant (11)
Cherry Garden Primary School

WOW!

We're the three wise men:
Casper, Melchior and Balthezar.
It started when we saw a star
Shining from afar,
It shone like a firefly in the night sky.

'Wow,' said Melchior.
'Cool,' said Casper.
'Amazing,' said Balthezar.

We felt that it was a dream come true,
So we travelled over desert and hill
To find the crown.

'Wow,' said Melchior.
'Cool,' said Casper.
'Amazing,' said Balthezar.

Jude Smith (11)
Cherry Garden Primary School

THE VISIT

I step down,
The dust goes everywhere,
But all I see is blue,
Like a never-ending swimming pool.
I see mountains and ragged rocks.
Volcanoes the colour of rust.
Sand with dotted brown crusts.
Volcanoes shoot fire,
The red flames,
Dissolve in the water.
I step forward,
I make my way to the edge of a plateau,
I take a deep breath,
All I see is rocks and rocks and rocks,
I fall.
I edge myself up,
My heart is beating,
I'm scared.
I want home.

Harry Webb (11)
Cherry Garden Primary School

I Am

I am a stylish and jolly girl.
I wonder if I'll ever become a dragon tamer?
I hear Jupiter and Earth smashing together.
I see a dragon jump for joy.
I want to glide over the moon on the back of my dragon.
I am a stylish and jolly girl.

I pretend to be a dragon taxi.
I feel the waves lapping my back as I ride along.
I touch the fire of the dragon.
I worry that I will be burnt one day.
I cry when my dragon gets hurt.
I am a stylish and jolly girl.

I understand that one day my dragon will die.
I say that all dragons live forever.
I dream that one day my dragon will have babies.
I try to be the best dragon trainer in the world.
I hope to love them all my life.
I am a stylish and jolly girl.

Marcella Pinto (10)
Colston's Collegiate Lower School

What I Did Today

I went to the doctor's today,
The doctor said to me,
'How is your tummy?
How is your head?
Have you eaten a flea?'

I went to the dentist today,
The dentist said to me,
'Have you been brushing your teeth lately,
And always after your tea?'

I went to the baker's today,
The baker said to me,
'Do you want a loaf of bread
Or sixty cakes for your tea?'

Esther Carter (8)
Colston's Collegiate Lower School

SCHOOL

I've been at Colston's since nursery
I think it's been good for me

Nursery was really fun
Even though we couldn't run

PP1 I was one of the bunch
A full day including lunch

PP2 We learnt a lot
About Roman cooking pots

PP3 We did lots of maths
Let's half things including paths

L1 We had Miss Tailby
She was really fair to me

L2 We had Mr Digby
He was just very funny

L3 Next to the science lab
A lot of things up for grabs

L4 I don't have much to say
So goodbye, and I'm off to play

Helena Stott (11)
Colston's Collegiate Lower School

SHE IS . . .

She is a delicate leather chair
She is a cunning fox
She is a very early day
She is a very bright yellow
She is an animal hospital
She is a bright T-shirt
She is cheese
She is a bright sunshine
She is a bright, hot holiday
She is jazzy music
She is Saturday
She is Scrabble
She is a pig book
She is my friend - Marcella.

Jaime Bracewell (10)
Colston's Collegiate Lower School

I WANT TO BE . . .

I want to be a bird,
To fly up high in trees,
But then again I might get shot
For all the hungerizee!

I want to be an elephant,
To lift my trunk up high,
But then again I might get dizzy
From looking up to the skies.

But no, not cats
They make me sneeze
And I don't want to have their fleas!

Alice Jess Carpenter (8)
Colston's Collegiate Lower School

I PUT IN THE POT . . .

Leg of a frog,
an ear of a dog.

A wing of a bat,
a talking hat.

A dragon's nail,
a dinosaur's tail.

A walking log,
a talking cat.

A dino baby's leg,
a baby dragon's wing.

A tail of a rat,
I'll put in that.

A toe of a cat,
How about that?

A skin of a bear,
Some children's hair.

Some poisonous potion,
some black beards, make-up water.

The Queen's daughter,
some blue water.

Some smelly socks,
some metal locks.

Some smelly feet,
an old seat.

Stir it around with a big round stick,
We're wicked witches, don't mess with us.

Emily Ebers (8)
Colston's Collegiate Lower School

A Cat

My mum, a long time ago,
Used to have a cat.
When it ate all its food
It turned ever so fat.

It played with a ball
It climbed up a tree
And when it came back
It had a flea.

She had a drink
It was milk
I got her brush
When I brushed her she felt like silk.

I cuddled her a lot
She had a nice bed
She would chase you all around the house
And she had a very fat head.

I was very sad
I had to take her to the vet
I was nearly crying
She looked so sorry, the sweet little pet.

I looked at the vet sadly
He had to put her down
Then I was crying
I did not frown.

Sophie Baber (9)
Colston's Collegiate Lower School

THE PEOPLE'S ALPHABET

A is Aaron who likes to play ball
B is for Bertie who is rather small
C is for Charlie who's got a pet newt
D is for Drummond who got stuck up a chute
E is for Emily whose friends are soft saps
F is for Freddy who likes wearing caps
G is for Gertrude whose singing is low
H is for Harry who sounds like a crow
I is for I'mbard whose body parts clank
J is for Jethro who thinks he's a tank
K is for Kim who runs market stalls
L is for Liam who plans to rob malls
M is for Michael who likes breaking lamps
N is for Norbert who collects lots of stamps
O is for Oscar who buys pencil cases
P is for Percy who fights us with maces
Q is for Queenie who talks in the class
R is for Robert who polishes brass
S is for Stevie who drinks all the rum
T is for Timmy who still sucks his thumb
U is for Una who bakes apple pies
V is for Victor who hangs out with spies
W is for Wilhelm who thinks he's the Kaiser
X is for Xerxes who plays with a laser
Y is for Yorrick, alas the poor soul
Z is for Zeanie who lives in a hole!

David John Fiander Stone (9)
Colston's Collegiate Lower School

I AM

I am a confident girl who loves horses
I wonder if I would ever be good enough
To jump the hurdles
I hear the horse's hoofs pounding the ground
I see a lovely golden horse running free in the woods
I want to ride on the beach, the air pushing against my face
I am a confident girl who loves horses

I pretend to be the best horse rider ever
I feel my hair billowing about as I ride in a lovely green meadow
I touch the sky as I jump over the hedge
I worry I might hurt myself
I cry when an animal dies
I am a confident girl who loves horses

I understand
I say let the horses run in the meadow
I dream about when I might get my own horse
I try to do what I'm told to do in lessons
I hope to ride when I want
I am a confident girl who loves horses

Stephanie Lewis (10)
Colston's Collegiate Lower School

JOHNNY

What are you doing Johnny, in the middle of May?
I am flying to a place a long way away.

What are you doing Johnny, down in the dump?
I'm watching ants crawl and elephants clump.

What are you doing Johnny, giggling a lot?
I have just seen a film called Dilling and Dot.

What are you doing Johnny, waving your hand?
I am saying goodbye to my castle in sand.

Claire Whyard (8)
Colston's Collegiate Lower School

I AM

I am naughty and love animals.
I wonder if the world will ever end.
I hear the animals calling me.
I see cavemen trying to use the square wheel.
I want to be older than I am.
I am naughty and love animals.

I pretend that I am a Victorian.
I feel every time I read a book I hear my heart thumping
Wondering what will happen.
I touch Pegasus, the winged horse.
I worry that people are ruining the atmosphere.
I cry that some people are going hungry.
I am naughty and love animals.

I understand we can't live forever.
I say that God made the world.
I dream I am the world's greatest artist.
I try to have neat handwriting.
I hope to some day seek success.
I am naughty and love animals.

Rowan Winstone (9)
Colston's Collegiate Lower School

I AM

I am a good boy who is very kind.
I wonder what technology will be like in 4000?
I hear waves crashing on a beach.
I see a sun-drenched beach with palm trees.
I want to be a millionaire.
I am a good boy who is very kind.

I pretend to be an airline pilot.
I feel that Christmas will never come.
I touch the sea in a sailing boat.
I worry about the hole in the ozone layer.
I am a good boy who is very kind.

I understand I won't live forever.
I say that forests should not be chopped down.
I dream that I live in the rainforest.
I try to behave.
I hope I live a happy life.
I am a good boy who is very kind.

Mark Edward Roberts (9)
Colston's Collegiate Lower School

THE GHOST IN THE ATTIC

In my attic I have a ghost called Fred
And he has a bed.
But just like me he drinks tea,
And on the bus he plays with us,
And he jumps in the sea with me.
And on Monday he went to sleep until Sunday.
Me and Fred have some fun together.
We'll be friends forever.

Alexander Beaves (8)
Colston's Collegiate Lower School

THE INGREDIENTS THAT GO INTO THE POT

A face of a dog and a log
A dragon's hair and a bear
A hat like a cat
A nice house, hair of a bat
A lion's scratch and a cat
A spider leg, a rat's bed
A dog's nail and a cat tail
A cat's blood and a slug
An old man's leg and a bed
Magic dust and wind gust
A magic leg like a small bed
A head of a frog, a leg of a dog
   I whizz it with a log
   To turn someone into a frog

Aimée Marshall (8)
Colston's Collegiate Lower School

ALLITERATION POEM

One weird whale wallowing in the water.
Two tornadoes twisting through a train.
Three thumbs thinking thumbs-up.
Four fat fingers fattening up.
Five filthy fish filling up.
Six silly snakes slithering stealthily.
Seven smelly socks snoozing in the sun.
Eight aprons aiming to aim eight aces.
Nine naive nuns nodding off.
Ten tangy ticks toddling terrifyingly.

Ross Martinovic (9)
Colston's Collegiate Lower School

MY MOTHER'S PREGNANT

My mother's pregnant.
What's she going to have, a girl or a boy?
I wonder.
My mother's pregnant.
What's the baby going to be like, good or bad?
I wonder.
My mother's pregnant.
What size is the baby going to be, big or small?
I wonder.
My mother's pregnant.
What if she's going to have twins or triplets?
I wonder.
What if I have to change its nappy. Yuck!
How do you do that anyway?
I wonder.
My mother's pregnant.
Is he or she cute?
I wonder.
Oh look who's here - it's Mum. She's back from hospital.
It's a girl, she's cute, she's good, she's small
And she's got a twin sister.
Ooooh Mum, she's just wet herself.

Abigail Nicole Litten (8)
Colston's Collegiate Lower School

RECIPE FOR REVENGE ON A BIG SISTER

Ingredients:
    A revising sister
    99% stressed
    A spoonful of annoying brother
    Access to a CD player or TV.

What to do:
>Firstly you make sure that the revising sister is next door revising,
>Then go to the CD player or TV.
>Turn it on and let it simmer.
>Finally turn the volume right up and let it melt in.

Kit Sheppard (10)
Colston's Collegiate Lower School

THE STONY SPELL

I put in the magic pot
A tail of a rat,
Face of a cat.
Man's leg,
Dog's head.
Hair of a polar bear,
The finger of the mayor.
Leg of an ox,
Eye of a Cyclops.
Heart of a bird,
Tin of lemon curd.
Beak of a parrot,
One whole carrot.
The biggest pest,
A nice guest.
The smallest star,
The biggest car.
Silly sea,
Silly me.
Stir it up with a bone to make a spell
Which will cast you to stone.

Eric Underwood (9)
Colston's Collegiate Lower School

A Recipe For Making Your Sister Jealous!

Ingredients: Nail varnish,
　　　　　　　　Lipstick,
　　　　　　　　Blusher,
　　　　　　　　Hair accessories,
　　　　　　　　Beautiful clothes,
　　　　　　　　High-heeled shoes,
　　　　　　　　Arrange a time to meet a beautiful boy.

What to do: Step 1. Wait until your parents have gone out the house.
　　　　　　　 Step 2. Start putting on make-up and find some nice clothes to wear.
　　　　　　　 Step 3. Tell your sister you've arranged to go out.
　　　　　　　 Step 4. Wait until he arrives and tell your sister you'll be back at 12.00pm.

Amelia Beaton (9)
Colston's Collegiate Lower School

What Am I?

I am a fruit.
I am round,
I have a stalk.
Sometimes I have a worm inside.
Sometimes I get peeled.
I am red and sometimes I am green.
Inside I am watery.
I can roll.
I have got pips inside.
I am juicy!

(Answer: An apple.)

George Lloyd (7)
Colston's Collegiate Lower School

PLAYTIME

The bell rings,
Everybody streams down the stairs,
The door crashes open,
Streams of children sprint out into the playground.

The black tar, roasting hot,
Enough to fry an egg,
The roar getting louder and louder,
The day as hot as a furnace.

The very small puddles exploding into steam
As balls hit them.
Little children bullied by big children.
Others playing happily.

Footballs flying around hitting people,
Teachers taking shade under trees,
Children playing rough and tumble on the grass,
The bell booms like church bells.
The torrent of children zooming back into the building,
Doors crashing closed.
Everything quietens down to silence.

Charles Hill (11)
Colston's Collegiate Lower School

WHALES

Whales swim in the sea
Whales flap their little tails
And whales are wet and slimy like little sea snails.
Whales blow out of a slimy air hole
That nearly blew a little crab away!

Annabel Paterson (8)
Colston's Collegiate Lower School

BEING PICKED ON

I walk out to break,
to see my doom.

I walk out and see the bullies,
I quickly try to hide.

They see me and run after me,
I retreat behind a car.

They hunt me down like hungry wolves,
they hunt in packs of six.

I look at my watch,
only two minutes to go.

Ding, ding, ding goes the bell,
I am saved by the bell once again.

Limping back to lessons cut and bruised,
I am so happy break's finished.

Thomas C A Fisher (11)
Colston's Collegiate Lower School

MUSIC

Music was quite boring,
Until there came L4,
Now I play the saxophone,
Which quickly shakes the floor.

I sometimes play the keyboard,
But I've never had a lesson,
So mum helps me learn a bit,
While dad's in relaxation.

I hope I get in a band some day,
It sounds like so much fun,
But the only problem really is,
I'm just a bit too young.

Peter Wollaston (11)
Colston's Collegiate Lower School

SCHOOL PLAY

Doors crash open
Children screaming
It's playtime!

Balls fly through the air
Tennis balls
Footballs
Why stop there?

Balls bounce high
Up and down
Side to side
Splash in puddles
On the boys' trousers.
Do they care?

Girls play chase
Talk and run
The wind blows through their hair.
Do they care?

The bell rings like thunder
The children aren't so happy now are they?
Now they're sad!

Emma-Claire Reed (10)
Colston's Collegiate Lower School

RUGBY MATCH

The two teams run out
Like lines of string.

To start the match a remote control car
Comes out with the tee
And the man kicks it higher
Than a big tree.

Mud slapped on people's faces
Ruks and malls and really big chases.

Vicious tackling, nippy running
Cautious passing and people saying,
'Why are the Scots dancing?'

The people need thrust because they are too slow
And they're being crushed.

The match has ended.
The score nil-nil and it was such a thrill.

William Brown (10)
Colston's Collegiate Lower School

THE SILENT RIVER

Tiny blue eyes gleaming up
From the mystery of the deep
Weeds droop
In the searing heat of the sun.

Fish leaping through the sheet of glass
On the top of the water
Shimmering with blurred secrets
Holding - holding - holding

Tiny blue eyes gleaming up
From the mystery of the deep
Weeds stiffen
In the frost of the moon

Daniel Watchurst (10)
Colston's Collegiate Lower School

SCHOOL WEEK

Monday is boring
You're tired from the weekend
The day goes so slowly
It drives you round the bend.

Tuesday's a bit better
The lesson I like is PE
We were to play squash
But Mr Digby forgot the key!

Wednesday's alright
RS is a chore
Sometimes the teacher
Tells you more and more and more.

Thursday's brilliant
'Cos I've got DT
But I hurt my finger
And everyone stared at me!

Friday's great
It's the end of the week
Oh no, I forgot
Detention for my cheek!

Rachael Moss (11)
Colston's Collegiate Lower School

THE RUGBY MATCH

Walk down quietly.
Tension building.
Pull boots on.
Jog up the pitch.
Up goes the ball, flying high, everyone charges.
The ball lands, everyone dives.
We fight hard but so do they.
Forty minutes of this will be such a drag.
Four minutes left and no score.
It was one of those days when it always was a draw.
The match report is going to be a bore.
Pull boots off.
Walk up quietly.

Jack Harris (11)
Colston's Collegiate Lower School

PESTS

A mouse a mouse is in our house,
It is eating all the cheese,
The little thing even gets past the cat,
Oh please.
A rat a rat is in our flat,
It even bit the cat,
When Mum sipped her tea,
Here comes some fleas.
They came in a rush,
Suddenly she sipped and caught the flea.

Julian Walcott-gordon (8)
Colston's Collegiate Lower School

ARE YOU SCARED OF THE DARK?

All is silent, all is well,
Except for the day, which has waved farewell.
Night is aware of what is around
And of what it has found.
It lures you where you never would go
And sometimes to places where you do know.
As the moon meets with night
The moon glitters on the sight.
And when the day sees the night
The moon yells, 'No, the light!'
Then they start to pick a fight!
The winner is . . . the night.

Now the monsters come to look.
As they creep through the forest to spook
The wind blows like a whistle
But be careful - it can catch you like a thistle!

When the night has had his fun
He swaps the moon with the sun.
That will be all for the night -
But *beware* - that was only for tonight.

Jamie FitzHenry (11)
Colston's Collegiate Lower School

THE WHITE SOCKS

White socks always get dirty,
Every time I wear them,
The longer I wear them the weaker they get,
Sometimes people say I should wash them every day!

Michael O'Reilly (8)
Colston's Collegiate Lower School

SCHOOL PLAYTIME

Lessons end, children screaming and shouting,
Corridors get busy with running children,
Teachers shout after the naughty ones,
When someone falls over the teacher sighs.

Children stand still to the whistle,
Vehicles drive on in,
Kids sneak inside,
Balls are thrown up high in the sky.

Children jump in puddles,
Balls land in puddles and get too wet,
The bell rings like a wedding,
They all stream inside.

All doors crash open,
The playground goes all quiet,
Then lessons start.

Sarah Vincent (10)
Colston's Collegiate Lower School

TEACHERS

Old teachers, young teachers,
Grumpy teachers, happy teachers,
Fat teachers, thin teachers,
Tall teachers, small teachers,
Hungry teachers, full up teachers,
Dirty teachers, clean teachers,
They are all fine for me.

Matthew Narey (8)
Colston's Collegiate Lower School

NIGHT

It's dark tonight.
I want to turn on the light
But I'm shuddering.
There's screeching and howling
And things are watching.

Things are hooting.
Things are scooting -
It's all creepy tonight.
I want to turn on the light
But I know I can't.

Eyes are looking
Shadows are flitting
It's all creepy tonight.
Oh so scary tonight -
I want to turn on the light!

Ashley Maggs (10)
Colston's Collegiate Lower School

TEATIME

My tea, my mother said,
Is very important to me.
But when I took a massive bite
It wasn't as nice as could be.
Then I gave it another try
And this time I shouted, 'Yippee!'
Because I turned the plate around
To finish off my tea!

Christopher Maggs (8)
Colston's Collegiate Lower School

AT SCHOOL

The clock strikes nine,
As I step into line.
The teachers all shout,
Because we were messing about.

We jog around the courts,
In our T-shirts and shorts.
Netball and hockey are fun,
But I prefer rounders in the sun!

The bell goes ring!
And our ears go ping!
We run up the stairs,
And sit in our chairs.

In geography,
It's a big yippee.
We get to watch,
The cool TV.

The lessons are over,
What's still to be done?
Too much, I'm afraid,
Time wasted in fun.

Harriet Campbell (11)
Colston's Collegiate Lower School

TWELVE LITTLE PRINCESSES

Twelve little princesses all with golden hair
Learning how to successfully cut a pear.

Twelve little princesses all with gleaming eyes
Learning how to successfully bake some pies.

Twelve little princesses all with skin like pearls
Learning how to successfully sail and swirl.

Twelve little princesses all with cloaks like trains
Learning how to successfully use some reins.

Shaun Malone (9)
Colston's Collegiate Lower School

DON'T YOU JUST HATE SCHOOL?

Getting dressed,
Is really hard,
When you're trying to look your best.

In the playground it's just the same,
Playing football,
It'll drive you insane.

For cricket I'm always on the bench,
I'd rather be learning,
Hordes of French.

In Maths I try not to get bored,
But in DT,
My grades have really soared.

Well, it's brilliant in lunch,
We ask for our food,
And start to munch.

When home time comes, I get to play,
But then I worry
About the next day.

Thomas Jelley (10)
Colston's Collegiate Lower School

A Witch's Spell

A piece of meat,
A smelly leg.
Eye of a dog,
Frog's leg.
Road Runner's head,
Coyote's leg.
Piece of a log,
Tail of a dog.
Some insects,
The lick of a chameleon.
Some baboon's blood,
Some mud.
Mix it with a spoon
To turn them into a baboon.

George Tucker (9)
Colston's Collegiate Lower School

Fireworks

Fire! Bang! Go the fireworks!
I like fireworks.
Red, blue, white, those are the colours of fireworks!
Enormous fireworks, small fireworks,
Whee! Go the fireworks.
Oh! Some people find fireworks interesting.
Round and round the Catherine wheel goes.
Kerbang they go!
Sky - they bang around, they go sailing into!

David Jackson (8)
Colston's Collegiate Lower School

EVIL SPELL

I put in the pot:

A piece of meat,
some smelly feet.
The leg of a dog,
the eyes of a hog.
A dinosaur's tail
and a little snail.
Some poisoned water,
the vicar's daughter.
An evil witch,
who is a snitch.

Mix it with a spoon
to turn you into
a fat, ugly baboon.

Jordan Underhill (8)
Colston's Collegiate Lower School

MY UNCLE JOHN

I have an Uncle John
I don't know where he's from
He follows Man U near and far
In his brand new motor car
He likes to wind us up
Then goes bye but
I love him very much.

Jayne Hulin (10)
Colston's Collegiate Lower School

SCHOOL DINNERS

At our school,
We have school dinners.

In the salad bar there is ham,
And custard as old as I am.
On Fridays we have hot dogs,
And for dessert we have choco logs.

Our lamb cutlet is so nice
We have some curry with some rice.
Our school dinners are really cool,
Or at least it's better than some gruel.
By the way, did you consider,
Having mash with liver?

Alex Underhill (11)
Colston's Collegiate Lower School

WHAT AM I?

I am round.
I am quite big.
I am hard and I am like a stone.
I grow underground.
You put me in a frying pan
Or a roast dinner.
I can be mashed.
I am browny-yellow
    And very muddy!

(Answer: A potato.)

Max Tarr (7)
Colston's Collegiate Lower School

MY TWIN BROTHERS

'Mum, it's my brothers again.
They're really bugging me.
Do you mind at all if I grind them in the grate?
Mum they're really annoying me!
It's just not fair.
Put them in the washer for a bit.
It'll teach them a lesson!
Oh Mum, they're so annoying.
Give them to a neighbour.
Oliver will like a change of scene.
William will say, 'That's just not fair'
Where are you taking me Mum?
Oh no, not my room.
What have I done wrong?
Have I been bugging you?'

Edward Philip (10)
Colston's Collegiate Lower School

FIREWORKS

Fireworks look like they're 3D.
If you run into a firework you could die!
Rushing fireworks, like a jet!
Enticing fireworks,
Working to entertain people.
October, one month to go!
Racing fireworks make the most noise.
Catherine Wheels go whiz around you!
Smash, crackle, *boom!*

James Laver (8)
Colston's Collegiate Lower School

CREEPY CASTLE

Door opens
heart beating
faster and faster
thump, thump, thump.

Fingers trembling
eyes in every corner
moon shivering.

Bells ringing
night glistening
stairs creaking.

Windows peeking
monsters lurking
monsters *creeping!*

Amy Lowndes (10)
Colston's Collegiate Lower School

FIREWORKS

Flashing in the sky, what a ride!
I love them.
Rushing in the sky, like a jet.
Exploring the sky.
Whoosh, through the sky.
Over our heads they fly.
Riding high,
Kind of wild.
Silence, it's over.

Samuel Ford (7)
Colston's Collegiate Lower School

My Mum

She gave birth to me,
She changed my nappies
When I was small.
She gave me a bath,
She changed my clothes.
My mum is best,
She is better than the rest.

She gives me a cuddle,
When I'm in a muddle,
That's my mum.

She cheers me up when I am sad,
She's brilliant at telling jokes,
That's my mum.

Harbhajan Singh Baryah (10)
Colston's Collegiate Lower School

Fireworks

Fireworks are noisy
Irritating fireworks
Roaring rockets
Everyone should be careful
We all had a lovely time
On November the fifth!
Roman candles
Keep well back
Sparklers can be fun!

Aaron Sealey Grant (8)
Colston's Collegiate Lower School

PETER PERFECT

There is a boy in my class,
Peter Perfect is his name,
And everything he ever does,
Only gets him fame.

It gets a bit up my nose, as sometimes,
No matter how hard I try,
I'll never be as good as him
And that is not a lie!

Still, I will keep on trying,
He won't be around forever,
And one day, when he is not there,
I might be even clever!

Aaron Farrel (9)
Colston's Collegiate Lower School

WHAT AM I?

I am an apple
I am green and eatable
I grow on trees
I clean people's teeth
I make the springtime
Look like stars gleaming in the moonlight
And in summertime I turn red and green
You pick me off a tree
I am juicy as well
And I am healthy.

Duncan Lambert (8)
Colston's Collegiate Lower School

THE STAFF ROOM (KEEP OUT)

The lair of the teachers, the pupils dread!

What's really going on in there?
Is it the home of Colston's undead?
Or the 'detention monster's' lair?

Some say it's all Jacuzzis and TV,
Some say it's a punishment cell.
Others say it's a gateway to Hell.

So when my mates and I sneaked in there,
When no one could see our intent.
We gasped at the tea and coffee there.
No sign of any grim punishment.

Teachers clearly enjoy their breaks,
Just like the girls and boys.
If you listen carefully
You'll hear they make the same noise!

Simon Charles Gilbert (11)
Colston's Collegiate Lower School

I PUT IN THE POT . . .

I put in the pot
Money and dummy, hail and tail.
A bell and shell, dogs and logs.
Jumpers and dumpers, plates and dates.
Snakes and cakes.
Mix with a bone to make someone into stone.

David Cruickshank (8)
Colston's Collegiate Lower School

SKIING

Skiing is sometimes scary
But also rather fun
Whizzing down the mountainside
With trees glittering in the sun.

The wind whistles past you
Your hair stands on end
It is a great experience
As you skid round a bend!

You're having a great time
You feel in control
Until you do a backflip
Straight into a hole.

Lying in a hospital bed
Is not much fun
But you can think of those memories
Skiing in the sun.

Tom Harris (11)
Colston's Collegiate Lower School

A WITCH'S SPELL

A monster, a lobster.
A tail of a dog, a face of a frog.
Some blood, some mud.
A twig, a pig.
A tongue, a mam.
Some arms and some alarms.

Maddy Thomas (8)
Colston's Collegiate Lower School

THERE WAS MY SILLY BROTHER

There was my silly brother of Beverly Road,
Who Mummy calls a lazy toad.

He sits around watching telly,
And all he does is fill his belly.

He never washes, so he's dirty still,
I think that's what makes him ill.

Even after all I've said,
I do not wish my brother dead.

I love him and he loves me,
Now I'm going to have my tea.

Katie Mason (10)
Colston's Collegiate Lower School

THE WITCH'S SPELL

I put in the cauldron . . .
A leg of a dog and the croak of a frog,
A dragon breathing fire burns the log.
A wing of a bat and a head of a cat.
The nasty screaming cry from beneath the pointed hat.
The snail's shell with a cat's tail.
The crashing sea as the whale sets sail.
Hubble bubble,
Toil and trouble,
Broken walls become old rubble.

Ashleigh Elizabeth Wayne (8)
Colston's Collegiate Lower School

NIGHT SHAPES

It was deep into the night.
It was dark and cold and wet.
You thought the trees were watching
Every move you made.

The grass shone in the moonlight
Like a silver glow.
You kept imagining that
Someone in front of you
Was scheming and planning
Your death - then suddenly
The someone
Disappeared into thin air.

Things were flying out of trees
Things were flying in your hair
Getting in the way of your running away.
And you were helpless.
Couldn't do anything
Until, at last, the air cleared . . .

Kyp Bridgen (11)
Colston's Collegiate Lower School

A POEM ABOUT ME!

I'm a skip and a jump from 26,
I'm short! I'm fat and round,
My name is Jay, I'm the youngest of three,
I live on the west side of town.
I like to play rugger with a bludger,
I eat lots of chocolate, fudge is my favourite.

Jay Drew (10)
Colston's Collegiate Lower School

Rugby

I like to play rugby, it's my favourite game,
No two matches are the same.
We often win, but sometimes lose,
The parents shout, 'Come on you Blues!'

My shirt is often covered in dirt,
I'm usually muddy and sometimes hurt.
I have lots of cuts and bruises too,
My legs are often black and blue.

I often think, night and day,
How we are all going to play.
Some of our matches are very tough
And we find the playing sometimes rough.

We finish our match and have a shower,
But we still feel full of power.
We have our tea just like young men,
Then we are ready to play again.

Stuart Bannerman (10)
Colston's Collegiate Lower School

The Street

Balls hitting cars
Kids eating Mars
Cats sleeping on walls
Birds screeching calls
Old grannies muffling
Hedgehogs rustling
Cyclists puffing
Motorists buffing

Jonathan Pickup (11)
Colston's Collegiate Lower School

MY FAMILY

My name is Aaron, I'm so cool,
I sometimes ride my bike to school.
I have a brother, he's alright,
I have a cousin, she just bites.
This brother of mine's called Ben,
He has no clue what I've done with his pen!
I also have a sister, she's never seven feet tall,
She always kicks and loses my ball.
Then there's my mum, she's sometimes sad,
So I try as hard as I can to make her glad.
This dad of mine, he's sometimes mad,
But only when his children are bad!
So here's my family big and small,
Unfortunately I'm still looking for my ball.

Aaron Burrell (10)
Colston's Collegiate Lower School

A BORING LESSON

The time never seems to go by,
I often wonder why?
The work seems really hard,
But really it's like making a card.
Others are working really well,
Why I can't, I just can't tell.
I am bored out of my brains,
I want to shut my book but I have to restrain
And now the bell has finally rang,
I close my book with a bang.

Miriam Mathieson (11)
Colston's Collegiate Lower School

A Trip To Oak Wood

People rushing to the door,
Taking out checks and many more.
Children sprinting for the big Black Hole,
The roller coasters fly swiftly through the air.
Adults eat, and go on the lazy dazy,
Whilst children . . .
Are running, playing, scared, screaming, soaring
And having a lot of fun.
The last ride is the booming go-karts.
People are ready for the big race.
After a long race and fun day, it was back home for me.

Andrew Croxson (11)
Colston's Collegiate Lower School

My Sister

My sister Nicole is annoying,
She messes up my room.
She mucks up my bed,
She makes my face go red.
I wish I had a brother instead!
A brother would be fun,
We could play with everyone.
Football, rugby, hockey,
PlayStation games too.
Yes, I think it would be good
To have a brother too!

Jonathan Mason (9)
Colston's Collegiate Lower School

SCHOOL RULES

School rules just never stop,
They make you feel,
Like you want to pop.
No balls in afternoon break,
Don't hang around,
You might be late.

When talking with a teacher,
Don't answer back,
Show them some manners,
Harsh voices they don't lack.

Be careful in maths,
You could get a detention,
But get lots of merits,
And you'll get a commendation.

Absolutely no one,
Can bring in lasers,
You must always wear,
Your nice, smart blazers.

Jenny Jones (10)
Colston's Collegiate Lower School

NIGHT

It's scary tonight.
I dare to turn out the light
And thick, black stillness
And weird shadows loom.

I dim the light.
I know I need it bright.
Wolves are howling.
Cats are scowling.

Figures are stealing.
Eyes are looking.
Night is brooding.
Morning is looming.

I wake up.
My light it out.
No funny shapes about.
Just the dark . . .

Andrew Beaves (10)
Colston's Collegiate Lower School

MY SISTER BETHANY

Home is where the heart is
Or that is what they say
But having to live with Bethany
I'd trade it any day.
She is my sister and I love her to bits
But please stop touching my lovely things
With your dirty, little mitts!
She's into all my make-up
And my school work too,
She's into all my CDs
And I never did find my right shoe.
Sometimes she makes me so angry,
I get really mad
But then she'll come and cuddle me
And that makes me feel so glad.
Home is where the heart is
Or that is what they say
But having to live with Bethany
. . . I wouldn't trade it any day.

Rebecca Whitehead (10)
Colston's Collegiate Lower School

MY FIRST DAY

On my first day
I had one friend
And I was worried
I would do things wrong.

On my first day
I was told
That Mr Watts
Gives lots of debits.

On my first day
I was told
That Miss Tailby
Gives lots of credits.

On my first day
I was told
That Mrs Whittaker
Gives lots of *merits!*

On my first day
I was told
We had to eat lunch
In the upper school.

On my first day
I was told
We were allowed to play
On the adventure playground!

Max Semple (10)
Colston's Collegiate Lower School

AT MY HOME AFTER SCHOOL

Every day after school,
We all come home, horrible and cruel.
It takes us half an hour,
Just to stop being sour.
It's the stress of the day,
With no time to play!

And as we go to tea,
We also watch TV.
We become a happy bunch,
When we start to munch.
Shouting dies down,
And yelling fades away.
But that's not the end of the day.
When everything is quiet,
A voice yells, *'Homework!'*

Peter Davies (11)
Colston's Collegiate Lower School

MY DAD

My dad is very mad!
I did something very wrong.
I took his shaver and split his blazer,
I started running round the house
And stood on his computer mouse.
Man, was he mad
And that was very bad
Because when he's mad
I get very sad.

William Olpin (10)
Colston's Collegiate Lower School

MY SCALEXTRIC

Today I'm going to see a car race,
There'll be a Focus and a Subaru there,
I bet the Focus will win.

So when we got to the race track,
The race had just begun,
At this point the Subaru was in the lead,
But then it drove the car straight off the track, into the sand.

So now the Focus was in first place
Zoom, zoom, zoom it went -
But then it slowed right down,
Oh! I see, he's crossed the winning line!

OK, so it was not a real race,
But it's still much the same,
On my Scalextric track in the garage
Where I can race them again.

Ben Krawiec (10)
Colston's Collegiate Lower School

MY COMPUTER

My computer lives on megabytes,
I thought it had a lot.
Now it seems to want some more,
I must have used a lot.

Oh no, it won't start up,
I think it needs a rest.
What now I ask, restore my back-up system?
I think it might be best.

I know what it may be,
The monitor's not switched on.
I press the button with a click,
But still the picture's gone.

Then to the rescue comes my dad,
He says he'll lend a hand.
What did he touch? It's working.
I just don't understand.

Samuel Gardiner (10)
Colston's Collegiate Lower School

TENNIS

I like playing tennis
It's really good fun.
I beat Jacob one time
Five-one.
I hit the ball as hard as I can
But I can't beat Jay though.
He's as good as Henman.
I run around the court
Whacking the ball,
I go for all the shots
But try not to fall.
At the end of the game, although I'm tired,
It's been really good fun!
Sometimes I win,
Sometimes I lose
But I like playing tennis.
It's the sport I would choose!

Ben Deeley (9)
Colston's Collegiate Lower School

DOLPHINS

Dolphins leaping all around,
Over the sea and then back down.
Splashing in the cold, blue sea,
Playing about like you and me.
    Splashing, jumping,
    Jumping, splashing.
I like dolphins!

Charlotte Alleyne (10)
Filton Avenue Junior School

THE SEA

The sea is like a bed of feelings,
Changing every day,
It twists and turns from coast to coast,
And has new things to say.

Its dangerous moves and stormy ways,
Are treasured just like gold,
You can't predict what it might do,
As its stories are untold.

Hannah Richards (11)
Filton Avenue Junior School

ZEBRAS, ZEBRAS

Zebras are black and white,
Eating their prey in the night,
Being hunted in dark and light,
Running and running with all their might,
After a while they're out of sight.

Adrian Price (11)
Filton Avenue Junior School

NUGGET THE SHEEP

Nugget the sheep
Lay sleepily on the grass,
His eyes gazing blankly,
His fluff floating in the wind.

He was caught,
Taken to the Blue Hawaii,
The sheep wonderland
(The slaughterhouse)

Not very bright,
He headed towards the mangle,
But out the end came a perfect sheep,
With the mangle crushed and broken.

The cooks were outraged,
They got lots of axes
To kill this one sheep,
But Nugget dodged and was gone.

When Nugget got home
The Druid sheep classed him
The Blue Hawaiian Prophet,
The first sheep to survive slaughter.

Nugget decided to save sheep
From burning houses,
From being lamb chops.
He taught them to save themselves.

Nugget the sheep
Lay sleepily on the grass,
His eyes gazing blankly,
His fluff floating in the wind.

Connor Smith (11)
Henleaze Junior School

FIVE WET SEA MONKEYS

Five wet sea monkeys,
Scurried along the sea floor.
A little one tripped over a rock,
Then there were four.

Four wet sea monkeys,
Looked out and saw a tree.
One tried to touch it,
Then there were three.

Three wet sea monkeys,
Couldn't find anything to do.
One jumped on its head,
Then there were two.

Two wet sea monkeys,
Found a giant gong.
One ran into it,
Then there was one.

One wet sea monkey,
Having anything but fun
Vanished without a trace,
Then there was . . . none.

Laura Sudworth (10)
Henleaze Junior School

HAIR

Hair can be tangly,
Hair can be straight,
Hair can be in different styles
Or just in a terrible state!

Hair can be so matted,
Hair can be in curls,
Hair can be styled
For boys and girls!

Zoe Jeffery (10)
Henleaze Junior School

THE MAGIC BOX

I will put in the box
The loud strike of lightning
The sparkle of a beautiful star,
And maybe the flame of a big, scaly dragon.

I will put in the box
The swish of a beautiful unicorn's mane
The whoosh of a wizard's wand.

I will put in the box
The smell of a lovely red rose
Or maybe the swish of a big green tree
Maybe the tropical animals of the rainforest.

I will put in the box
A splashing, excited dolphin in the sea
A lovely yellow beach with lots of shells.

It will be polished silver with golden locks
And a lid made of stars.

I will jump the highest jump
On my pony in my box.

Charlotte Husher (9)
Henleaze Junior School

FIRE

Red-hot fire,
Burning down the house,
No one can hear it, not even a mouse.
Flames creeping up the stairs,
No one knows, so no-one cares.

Little matches might start it,
A candle or scented stick.
Oil burner, cooking, maybe just a flick.
Lighter, cigars and glass,
Catching onto the green grass.

Blazing wood fire,
Speeds through the trees,
And afterwards nothing.
Just black, cindered ashes.

George E Day (10)
Henleaze Junior School

RIVER SOUNDS

Swishing, swirling, swerving,
The river turns and twists,
Swirls, swooshes, swishes,
With currents it meanders carefully around rocks.

Splash, splish, splash
Children paddle
Swiftly, slowly, silently
Fish swim around fishing net.

Eleanor Head (10)
Henleaze Junior School

BATTLEFIELD

What do you see in a battlefield?
Dead men, aeroplanes,
Smashed up houses and windowpanes.
That's what you see in a battlefield.

What do you hear in a battlefield?
Bang here, crash there,
Missile launches everywhere.
That's what you hear in a battlefield.

What do you feel in a battlefield?
Bruises, cuts, broken leg,
Anger, pain, the longing to be fed.
That's what you feel in a battlefield.

Jared Stride (9)
Henleaze Junior School

DIRECTIONS

Left, right, right, left,
Up, down,
Sideways, round,
Topsy-turvy, inside out,
In ways, out ways,
All around.

This way, that way,
Inside out,
Back to front,
Over and out.

Matt Jones (10)
Henleaze Junior School

ARRRR WITH A CAPITAL A

I'm going to my new school today
My teacher's called Miss Brown,
She hates people who smile
And loves people who frown.

And if you're being kind
She will totally explode,
And she won't let you out of the classroom
Without saying the magic code.

She feeds you with green soap
And one rabbit dropping,
Adding five marshmallows
And ketchup for a topping.

And now it's the end of the day
After hours of war,
I'm standing very patiently
She wishes me a good day through the door!

Abigail Smith (10)
Henleaze Junior School

LIGHT

L ight is bright and flickers in front of the eyes,
I t is fierce but peaceful.
G lowing quite bright with a welcoming feeling,
H ot as it is it is still serene.
T he light means peace to me which should be on Earth.

Simon Foale (9)
Henleaze Junior School

MY KITTEN

I'm going to get a cat,
Not any old cat is that.
A kitten it will be,
As you plainly see.
It will be cuddly and kind,
As you would certainly find.
I'll feed it every day,
And with it I will play.
I'll stroke it behind its ears,
And try to loosen its fears.
I'll always look for fleas,
Our love would never cease.
I'll love it so,
And hope it would never go.
I'm getting a kitten soon,
Just wait and see!

Sophie Buchanan (11)
Henleaze Junior School

LIGHTNING

Striking through the cold, bleak sky,
Never covered by the clouds so high.
Drums of thunder, ganging,
Zigzagging lightning, hanging,
Yellow golden streaks falling,
Thunder, who is it calling?

Claire Sangster (10)
Henleaze Junior School

ELEPHANTS

Elephants go thud, thud, thud
As they squelch through slimy mud.
A creature lifts its trunk up high
And makes a noise I can't describe.
A noise like 1000 trumpets sounding
A noise like 1000 winds all howling.
I put my hands tight over my ears
And hoped that I would never hear
A noise quite as loud
As the elephant's terrific sound.
Though I am not surprised at all
That a beast so big and tall
Can make a noise just like this.
It's probably for him perfect bliss!

Robbie White (10)
Henleaze Junior School

THE SEA

The crashing waves upon the shores,
The shipwrecks under sea.
The dark night sky with grey, dull clouds,
Then clear morning breeze.
The huge, grey sharks with pointed teeth,
The cold, bleak weather.
The sailors jumping overboard,
The sunken, heavy treasure.

Carla Ahmadi (10)
Henleaze Junior School

LIGHT

Candles burning clearly in the darkest room,
Shedding light around them,
Brightening up the gloom.

Driving past the street lamps,
In the darkest night.
Brightening up the highway,
With their shimmering light.

Swimming in the sunshine,
Bathing off the shore.
Seeking sparkling seashells,
To hear the waves roar.

Benedict Campbell (9)
Henleaze Junior School

SNOW

Snow thickly matted,
Glittering, sparkling like it has tinsel buried inside.
Birds digging for food,
Animals trying to find shelter for the cold night.
Crackling, crunching when footsteps pass,
It slides heavily from the roof to the ground.
Snow deadens any sound.

The day gets warmer and jolly snowmen start to shrink.
Green patches start to appear in gardens and parks and fields.

The snow has gone.

Katie Andrews (9)
Henleaze Junior School

SNOWFLAKE

Settling on the window,
Melting on the ground.
Sliding down the rooftop,
Ready to be found!

Eating up the autumn,
Melting in the sun.
Turning into puddles,
Then your snowflake's gone!

Like stars they fall from snow-white skies,
Then snowball fights we play.
But then we stop for snowflakes melt,
Oh what a lovely day.

Saskia Daller (10)
Henleaze Junior School

HEAVEN GATES

The door of Heaven stood wide open
Waiting to swallow me in
The arch encrusted with jewels
Opals, emeralds, rubies and sapphires
And inside the gate
I could see
People in white glimmering gowns
Glittering in joyful, happiness
The stars were shining softly
And the moon was bright
Yes, I will never forget that day I entered Heaven.

Sophie Mason (8)
Henleaze Junior School

FIREWORKS

Whizzing, spinning all around,
In the starry glow.
What firework will come up next?
It's impossible to know.

Rockets, bangers, Catherine wheels,
In the midnight sky.
The bangers are exploding,
Reaching up so high!

Children waving sparklers,
Underneath the moon.
The fireworks have ended now,
Why did they finish so soon?

Catharine Hiley (10)
Henleaze Junior School

THE RED ROSE

The lovely red rose
The red, red rose
Is a she
Who dances like a ballerina

Her long, slender stalk sways
In a light breeze
Her thorns are as sharp as spears

Her delicate petals make
A crown for her head

Caitlin Barnbrook (9)
Henleaze Junior School

SPRING

Spring, spring, wonderful spring
the dew is on the leaves.

Spring, spring, wonderful spring
the fairies come out and play.

Spring, spring, wonderful spring
the sun is shining like a great ball of fire.

Spring, spring, wonderful spring
the barbecues are burning.

Spring, spring, wonderful spring
the trees and green leaves.

Spring is wonderful.

Melissa Catalano (8)
Henleaze Junior School

THE NIGHT OF GOLD!

Shimmering, glimmering in the night
the moon was still and fairies bright.

The children sleeping softly lay
their dreams beautiful and fey.

The rain was soon to be here
the animals curled up quite near.

The whispering bushes, the icy air
the midnight trees were twirling fair.

So if you see the night of gold
beware, it's true gold I swear.

Emily Thompson (8)
Henleaze Junior School

DRAGON

O dragon how wonderfully you soar.
Higher than a cascading waterfall,
Beneath the crack of wailing thunder,
And far above a cave, ready to be plundered.

O your glowing, fiery scales,
Your life, repeated in tales,
From generation to generation you have been feared
By traveller to army which have all steered
Away from your lair in the mountain caves,
As you shall defeat them, wave by wave.

O dragon, your marvellous complexion,
Those sockets as eyes and those razor-like talons,
And that fire you cast is like a river of red,
Standing majestically is your powerful head.

O dragon, O dragon I wonder why
Your masterful wings propel you so far in the sky?
O dragon what a form you take!
Slain only by the depths of a lake . . .

David Wilkinson (11)
Henleaze Junior School

MY UNUSUAL DOG

A tail like a whip,
And paws like boxing gloves.
Its body like a bag of bones,
Its howling like a baby.
Its nose like a dung beetle.
Its teeth like Dracula's fangs.

Christian George (9)
Henleaze Junior School

THE CAT

The cat stalks proudly,
Round the darkened city,
Its vibrant eyes skimming around every corner.
As he strolls, cats all around him pass by without a word.
Swiftly on he padded,
Past dark alleyways, brightened street lights till,
Vrooooommmm!
His back arches,
Fur sticks up,
He stands stock still.
Soon a car comes shooting past,
Spraying him in a slosh of water,
A hiss breaks out and he slinks off in the other direction,
Heading for home.
His bedraggled fur sticking up at odd angles.
Silently he rounded a corner and *crash!*
He bounds through his cat flap and into his cosy bed of warmth!

Charlotte Russell-Smith (10)
Henleaze Junior School

COOKING

Scrambled eggs and chicken's legs.
Fry things, boil things, roast things, toast things.
Throw in a rack of meat, make it go down like a treat.
Hey, there's some egg to beat, make the scallops very neat.
Have some Sunday roast tonight, have ghost cookies for a fright.
Have some beef, lick it clean, cook some dinner with margarine.
Cook the veggies so they're green, make the cooking food supreme.

Henry Phillips (10)
Henleaze Junior School

ON SAFARI

I'm on the safari,
And what do I see?
I see a crocodile,
Snapping like a mouse trap,
I go on deeper in,
And what do I see?
I see a brave lion standing in my way,
I try to run away,
But it's too fast.
It could run as fast as a speeding bullet.
I make it back to the car and I get in.
I hear a crunching sound.
Paws or feet running away.
I get out.
I look at the back of the rock hard car.
I looks like a lion had bitten the back of it.

Jennifer Brierley (9)
Henleaze Junior School

WORLD WAR II

As the war begins, the aircrafts glide to the battlefield.
The soldiers say their last words and a prayer to their families,
Then start to march to the battlefield.

As the planes are crashing, the men are dying,
The mine bombs are blowing, death is rising,
Families crying, trees falling,
Faith disappearing, houses demolished,
Millions of lives destroyed.

Adel Chowdhury (9)
Henleaze Junior School

SHOES

There are
Red shoes
Black shoes
White shoes
Blue,
Shiny shoes
Scruffy shoes
Old shoes
New,

Strong shoes
Weak shoes
Stubborn shoes
Boots,
Trainer shoes
Big shoes
Tight shoes
Loose.

Elena Deakin (9)
Henleaze Junior School

THE WINTER HORSE

I saw that winter horse, in the winter snow.
'I haven't seen it of course, it's just a horse.'
It isn't just a horse, it's a winter horse.
It's dark brown with snow-coloured dots on its forehead,
And every night I dream of it.
It seems real.
And as I saw it was wrapped in snow,
It looked as white as a white frosted blanket.

Sophie Fletcher (8)
Henleaze Junior School

Pandora's Box

Hermes came flying over the beautiful land
A treasure chest type box clutched in his hands
He descended down to the paved concrete
And landed slowly, the ground rested at his feet
Pandora's mansion was his destination
Her wedding present was this wonderful creation
He found the house and was invited inside
Pandora and her husband were told not to open the box and peep inside
Although Hermes knew they'd be beside themselves with temptation
To open up this fantastic creation
A few weeks later Pandora couldn't resist
But to open up her treasure chest
What was inside? She would wonder
Every time she saw the chest that was what she would ponder
As quick as a flash, she opened the box
But there were no jewels or pretty frocks
Only the voices saying, 'I am Pain,' 'I am Disease,'
'I am Disappointment,' 'I am Greed,'
They changed the world in every possible way
There were no more relaxing days
Pandora slammed the lid of the chest down
Slowly, she knelt down to the ground
With tears tumbling down her cheeks
She heard a soft, sweet voice speak
'Let me out, let out, I can change it all.'
'What?' asked Pandora, reluctantly opening the box once more
Out rose a stunning silver butterfly
She smiles, 'Pandora, don't you cry
For I am Hope, have faith in me
I will change the world, just you wait and see.'

Sophie Stephens (10)
Henleaze Junior School

MY STAR VOYAGE

Up, up, up to the stars,
There goes Mercury, there goes Mars.
We're flying higher, higher still,
There's a black hole ready to kill.
We're going down and down and down,
Oh I feel such a clown.
I'm stuck up here in mid-air,
As if I'm held up by my hair.
In my spacesuit I stay put,
Though I can hardly lift my foot.
Our voyage is complete,
Get back in your seat.
On a star we have stepped,
Walked, jumped and leapt.
My time in space is up,
I'm going to my home.
My time in space is up,
Look, I can see the Dome.

Hannah Cooper (10)
Henleaze Junior School

THE NIGHT BEFORE CHRISTMAS

We were waiting, waiting for it to happen.
The flames dancing in the frosty moonlit air
As though they were alive.
Our stockings were hanging by the burning fire,
Swinging back and forth like a rocking horse
In a nursery, empty and dull.
In the cold night air an owl hooted a warning to her chicks.
The clock struck, and I drifted off to sleep.

Jenny Croker (8)
Henleaze Junior School

THE POLE HOUSE

Forty-three steps lead to the glass-stained door.
You enter, and look down into a sunset-stained harbour.
The bridge glows like an everlasting rainbow.
Back inside a small fat dog in a woven basket gives a small
        contented bark.
Your room, a small mattress and a lovely view.
A chest of drawers planted in a corner.
A small fire burning in the cosy living room.
And an old grandfather clock collects dust all year round.
Under the table I crawl
And see breadcrumbs scattered, amidst the dog's hairs.
Leaving is like someone has died, nobody wants to go.
It's raining cakes, and a goodbye bark echoes in the background.

Louise Jones (8)
Henleaze Junior School

RAIN

Drip, drop on the ground,
Rivers rushing all around,
Squish, squelch in the mud,
Oh no, it's starting to flood.

Splish, splosh in the puddles,
Under umbrellas people in huddles,
Pitter, patter of the rain,
Will the sun come out again?

Trickling down the windowpane,
Water running down the drain,
Hooray the sun's come out today,
Now we can go out to play!

Katie White (10)
Henleaze Junior School

LITTLE KITTEN

The kitten, the majestic kitten,
Strides across the plain old city
Showing off his ten exquisite colours of rage,
That show as his fur stands up in the wind bow.
His stealth, thrusts across the street
Dark colours, that creep down his spine, and as his gentle sleeps
That come now and then, the sun rises and shine in heaps
That's burning hot and he wakes, oh the smell of wine,
He trudges on perfectly fine!
When he's stroked he approves with a purr
As the hand flattens his delicate fur
His soft, gentle paws move
Steadily onwards, his smooth
And cute little head
Of hair, his sleek undersized body unfed.
His vibrant colours, his extremely sharp teeth,
His gentle appearance hid well underneath.
The hurtful, sore alley cats petrify him,
The little kitten, and soon he lost the sparkle in his eye.
He snatches at everything he can slash his paws on
His silent, stealth feelings stay on as one.
And then he arrived, a master of fame.
The kitten grew faster
With all his luxurious food
And that's the end of a kitten named Dude.

Richard Foale (11)
Henleaze Junior School

NOBODY WANTS ME!

I'm bashed and bruised as I fall to the soil,
Nobody wanted me back in the packet,
They were pushing and shoving like swords in a battle.

Now I am happier down in the soil,
Stretching and growing till I first see light,
I am enjoying my first stages of metamorphosis,
Wondering what I will be.

I have green leaves growing now,
A white top, almost as white as snow,
I waver about in the wind.
I'm a cauliflower
And nobody wanted me back in that packet.

And now I am thinking as I travel,
Down the road in a bumpy old cart,
Was it such a good idea to be a cauliflower?
And the other seeds, are they thinking the same,
Or getting on with life?

I'm in the fridge still thinking,
It's almost as cold as the North Pole,
Somebody's coming for me,
I'm going to the pot, no I'm not,
I'm going to the compost,
I wondered what that green fluff was on my head,
Nobody wants me!

Rebecca Heryet (11)
Henleaze Junior School

BATH TIME

First it was the itching,
Then came the scratching.
Then came the *bath!*

'Your dog has fleas!' the neighbour shouted.
(But that, of course, *I* seriously doubted.)
I hated baths - the bubbles, the soap.
I tell you, I just cannot cope,
With scrubbing until I'm almost furless.
Next they'll put my hair in curlers!

'Come on now Fluffy!' my master's daughter yelled.
And the next thing I'm being held!
Woah! The water's freezing cold.
Your paws turn to ice I was told
By the bulldog who lives across the street.
(We often go to the park to meet.)

But anyway, I tell you now,
The shampoo hit me, *Kapow! Kapow!*
The bubbles went right up my nose,
So I splashed all my master's clothes.
He jumped away and looked quite mad.
(It actually made me feel quite sad).

'You mangy dog! I can't stand this
So now we must quite dismiss
The idea of you being given a bath.'
(Although it was quite a laugh).
So peace at last, the fleas are dead,
And I'm left to roll in the flowerbed.

Harriet Buckner (10)
Henleaze Junior School

THE ROCKET

The Rocket
needs mushroom
fuel
'Check.'

The Rocket
needs a capsule
that fires popcorn
'Check.'

The Rocket
needs a
sealed capsule
'Check.'

'5, 4, 3, 2, 1
we have lift-off.'

Five hundred feet
through the sound barrier
through the ozone layer
into outer space

'It worked.'
'Yes!'
'Release capsule.'

On the very dangerous
journey

'Look! There's the UK.
A pea with blue splodges.'
'I can see my house.'
'Don't be stupid.'

William Rowe (8)
Henleaze Junior School

THE BATTLE OF MARATHON

In response to the Ionian uprising
Darius sent a great army comprising
Twenty-five thousand Persians - archers and infantry
(In battles they'd always had victory)
To the city of Marathon.

The Athenians, fearing a bruising,
Sent to Sparta for help - these refusing
Left Athens to face the Persian horde
Armed with bow and arrow, javelin and sword
On the plains of Marathon.

Though outnumbered and lacking in cavalry,
Miltiades employed a new strategy:
Head-on, they attacked, with a roar
Leaving the Persians dead on the floor
At the battle of Marathon.

More than six thousand Persians were slaughtered
And Darius' vengeance was thwarted.
The Athenians had won a great victory,
Which went down in the pages of history
Following the battle of Marathon.

Pheidippides ran with delight
To Athens to tell of the fight.
When he got there, he died,
But his last words he'd sighed
About the victory at Marathon.

Herodotus wrote down the story
To celebrate Athens' glory.
A temple was built called the Parthenon,
In thanks for the victory at Marathon
For the glorious victory at Marathon.

William Jenkinson (& his parents) (8)
Henleaze Junior School

SITTING ON THE STREET

Sitting on the street,
Begging for some money,
1p, 2p, 3p, 4p?
Or maybe something yummy?

Sitting on the street,
Looking for some scraps,
Any old garments?
Or warmer clothes perhaps?

Sitting on the street,
Never read a book,
Freezing in the corner,
Don't you ever look?

Sitting on the street,
Please, please help me!
I'm as poor, as poor,
Don't you see?

Rebecca Shuttleworth (8)
Henleaze Junior School

WHIRLWIND

Fat, glittering snowflakes slowly drifting down
Lightning flashing up above the ground
White, wet snow falling from the sky
And small, cold icicles hanging from the caves
The sharp, bitter snow making you cringe
This can only mean one thing

Whirlwind.

Jessica Ardis (9)
Henleaze Junior School

THE DREADED MATHS TEST!

I sit there biting my nails,
As she hands out all the sheets,
I can feel myself shaking,
While she sets the clock for an hour,
I'm really nervous,
She tells you to start,
I work through it quickly,
Though I'm sure I got some wrong,
Then the buzzer goes, it's time to stop,
I go out to break,
Hoping I got some right,
I go back into the classroom,
Feeling my face get hot,
She goes through the answers,
Then tells us what we all got,
I got 70/76 *Yyyippppeeee!*

Jenny Nicholls (9)
Henleaze Junior School

DADS

Fat dads
Thin dads
Mine's the best
Small dads
Tall dads
And the rest
My dad's the strongest
And he is
The one in the world that you want to kiss

Emily White (8)
Henleaze Junior School

TIME TRAVEL

I travel, back in time,
It's so sublime.
Shakespeare's using,
Lots of rhymes,
He writes plays,
And stories too,
One about me,
And one about you.

Flying cars,
And floating bars,
Then everybody's eating,
A new type of Mars,
There's more games to play,
But I prefer the present day.

Mahdi Shariff (11)
Henleaze Junior School

CHRISTMAS EVE

Snow is drifting gently down to the house
While I sit back in my comfortable armchair at six o'clock.
I look up to the rainbow-coloured sky.
I see the moon smiling right up high.
I listen to my favourite music 'Silent Night'.
When it's nine I go up to put up my stocking,
As red as a ruby.
I wait and I wait till morn.
Snow is drifting gently down to the house,
Christmas Day dawns.

Polly Northam (9)
Henleaze Junior School

I'D LIKE TO BE...

I'd like to be a millionaire,
And win one million pounds.
I'd like to be a football player,
And score the only goal.
I'd like to be a basketball player,
To score for our team.
I'd like to be a teacher to teach,
And teach all day.
I'd like to be a babysitter,
To babysit all day.
I'd like to be famous,
And write a poem like this!

Isabelle White (8)
Henleaze Junior School

THE SLEEP BOY AND HIS BROTHER

Every night at dusk
The sleep boy flies overhead
Casting his velvet blanket
Over the world
Sending people to sleep

Then comes his little brother
Casting dreams over the sleeping children
And their parents
Together they fly lonely over the world
Lonely and homeless
Leaving sleep and dreams behind them

Jonathan Appleby (9)
Henleaze Junior School

THE PONY

The pony down the road is lovely
He twirls like a sun beaming
His colours are a creamy brown
As rich as the colours of the sun
He gallops as fast as a satellite
His hooves paw at the ground
As he grinds up mud and gnaws at grass
Which has turned a sickly yellow colour
When he neighs he runs to greet me
For he knows when we dance
Like a bird soaring through the bright blue sky
I love him and he loves me and I know that he does.

Rosalind McClelland (8)
Henleaze Junior School

THE KITTEN TO THE CAT

At first they are as wet as water,
Then they are so fluffy they remind me of a toy.
As they see what is all around them,
They start to explore the home.
They have their food and have a rest,
As they get older and older
They become cats, they are massive
And are quite overweight.
Most of the time they are sleeping
And never want to have fun.
They just want a quiet corner
For the rest of the day.

Philippa Campbell (11)
Henleaze Junior School

The Sunflower

The beautiful yellow flower petals dance gracefully in the wind
Like a ballerina performing
Its bright, green leaves are feathers fluttering about
The big stalk, standing mighty strong like a soldier armed with spears
Ready for battle
But
What stands out most of all is the pollen
The flower blossoms at sunrise
Growing, growing
The sunflower does until
It is a five-foot tall, friendly giant
But still
Dances gracefully
Not a bit better
Not a bit worse

Josephine Holloway (9)
Henleaze Junior School

Caterpillar

I am a little egg,
as happy as can be.
I am growing legs now,
6, 5, 4, and 3.
I think it's time to go inside,
my little nest cocoon
and when I come out,
as a butterfly,
I'll fly, fly, fly away.

Lucy Catherine Rowe (10)
Henleaze Junior School

MASTERPIECE

Miss Bookworth's blaring on at us,
Like the sea crashing onto the rocks!
'Hannah,' she suddenly yells.
I sit up straight and stare at her.
'Yes Miss!' I say,
Sounding as if I know what she's talking about.
'Pay attention now,' she announces.
Knowing better I don't reply.
She carried on about a poem,
No, now we have to write one.
I'm hopeless at rhyming,
I'm terrible with words.
I'm not good at any subject!
I grab the thesaurus,
Take every word I can.
There, it's finished, now to hand it in.
But I just get sent back to my seat.
Alright, I'll try properly now . . .
I actually get a 'well done' from Miss Bookworth,
And my poem's up on the wall.

Hannah Levene (11)
Henleaze Junior School

THE KITTEN

It is like a small slithery seal when it slowly emerges.
Then it becomes a fluffy mischievous ball.
It reminds me of a cute, cautious, cuddly toy, small and round.
Then it learns to be devoted to its owner.
After that it becomes a fantastic mouse catcher.

Kelcy Harvey (10)
Henleaze Junior School

PUPPY

Puppies are so fluffy
They have the cutest face
They come in different colours
And they like to play and race
They move as swiftly as a bird flies
They eat as quick as a cheetah runs
They fetch a stick as quick as a tick
They run as fast as a frog leaps
And they bark as loud as a lion roars
I like them as they are
They are so cute and fluffy
I can play with them anytime
Because they don't bite me
That is my lovely puppy Rascal.

Hannah Lewis (10)
Henleaze Junior School

THE CHEETAH

I start to run when the sun comes out.
I get tired because I run in circles like a roundabout.
I eat like a hungry bug
With blood and guts round my mouth.
I ask the female cheetah for a hug
Then I play a game of cards.
I win because I cheat.
I hold the best cards between my toes.
No one will find out because I'm the only one who knows.
Soon it's almost night.
The sun is setting and it's a very pretty sight.

Gene Jozefowicz (10)
Henleaze Junior School

THE BULLET

Bang, it goes.
It's like an eagle in the sky,
Not caring what it hits.

It finds the target,
It won't turn back.
It is not scared,
Just don't get hit.

Finally it hits,
Ripping through the skin like a chainsaw through a tree.
There's no time to move,
Just hope you don't get hit.

Jack Radford-Sidney (11)
Henleaze Junior School

WASTING TIME

Miss, can I go to the toilet?
And I can't find my book.
I lost my pen, Miss.
And now I've found it, it's run out and my pencil is blunt.
Brian keeps poking me, Miss, what shall I do?
My page is scrumpled up like an old man's face.
I'm hot, Miss, the sun is in my eyes
So can I open the window please, oh please.

So, ooo do I have to start again?

Yes oh yes.

Rosamund Thomas (8)
Henleaze Junior School

THE ELEPHANT

The long fat body of the elephant, walking across the Indian plains,
Its leather skin, swirling around its body like wind in its leaves.
His long, dangly trunk hanging down from its face of wrinkles and long
    ivory tusks.
Slowly grabbing hold of bushes and uprooting small trees
And crunching them in its big mouth,
And the sound of little animals running away from this gigantic beast.

The elephant thunders over the land, and petrifies humans and
    animals alike,
He drinks gallons of water as though they were mere millilitres,
And then spurts it out of that long trunk, that is miles long.
The other animals cower in fright and as they do so they think of:

    The elephant.

Matt Quaife (10)
Henleaze Junior School

WHO WANTS TO BE A MILLIONAIRE?

Who Wants To Be A millionaire
I sit and watch every night, just sit and stare.
If someone becomes a millionaire,
I dream of money flying through the air.
You say, 'I thought this day would never come true,'
As Chris Tarrant hands a cheque to you.
A cheque for £16,000 or more,
You just go rushing out the door.
You look at the cheque . . . it's only for £1!
You stop and faint down to the ground.

Helen White (10)
Henleaze Junior School

AT CAMP

The sun was shining on a hot, hot day
Out in the camp's meadows to play
Having fun with my favourite games
Skipping down the near dusty lanes

As fast as an ostrich I went
Until I found my tent
Sitting alone reading a book
Then my mum came in and gave me a surprised look

Starting to tuck into bed
Trying to rest my tired head
Having really good dreams
As the sun's yellow beams
Start to go down
I have dreams of my own home *town*.

Anna Barham (8)
Henleaze Junior School

SNAKE

This fiendish hunter of scaly appearance,
With a mischievous nature and love of disaster,
His vicious lifestyle will stop at no ends,
His skill in night hunting, of this he's the master.
Rat or mouse, rabbit or hare,
Of this horrific fate . . . beware.
In short terms:
If prey is spotted by eyes jet black,
Too late, it's gone . . . *it won't come back!*

David Cutler (11)
Henleaze Junior School

TIMETRAVELLER

I'm going on a voyage
through the web of time.
Some images are gory
but some are quite sublime.

First up is the Stone Age
with caves and dinosaurs.
Where man's primitive brain
couldn't even open doors.

Next up is the Egyptians
with the mighty river Nile.
With pharaohs, sphinxes and pyramids
it's got to make you smile!

Third is the Romans
the conquerors of their day.
With the mighty Emperor Caesar
who would always have his way.

Next up is Adolf Hitler
in the Second World War.
Battling at Dunkirk
with plenty of gore.

Now I've travelled through time
and seen all I must see.
Now from this poem you must know
my favourite subject's history!

Jonathan Maszuchin (11)
Henleaze Junior School

LAZY AND IDLE

My bedroom's a mess,
The curtains aren't pulled,
My bed isn't made,
But I don't care!

I don't listen at school,
I lie around at home,
I don't do my homework,
But I don't care!

I jump on my bed,
To watch TV,
I play loud music,
But I don't care!

I'm a dirty old brat,
My clothes are full of holes,
I don't take baths,
But I don't care!

My hair is all scruffy,
My laces are undone,
They're also scuffed,
But I don't care!

I've got scars on my face,
Warts on my feet,
My nails are too long,
But I don't care!

Wahey, what a life!

David James Benjamin Clark (9)
Henleaze Junior School

THE SQUIRREL

Scampering up a tree,
Bounding across the leafy ground,
Leaping away, branch to branch,
Sniffing the air to see,
The great monstrosity behind me,
Crashing through the trees,
The huge mouths snapping here and there,
The light flitting through the branches,
I'm running away, I try to escape,
I think I've just about made it,
I'm out of the forest finally,
And I look behind me,
That great big digger,
Killing all the trees.

Matthew McCoubrey (10)
Henleaze Junior School

MY NEW BABY SISTER

When my new baby sister was first born,
I came home to see her on that wonderful morn.
I gave her a cuddle but she didn't peep,
For the next few days all she did was sleep.
But after some time she changed her ways,
She didn't stay *so quiet* after those first peaceful days.
She screamed all night,
Gave the neighbours a fright,
Though when they looked, she was a very cute sight.
When my new baby sister was first born,
I came home to see her on that wonderful morn.

Kyana Wambui Gitahi (10)
Henleaze Junior School

THE STRANGEST DREAM

I had the strangest dream last night
that I have ever had
I dreamt of 100 steps that I had to climb
and every step that I took out came a surprise
behind doors, up chimneys, down holes and a lot more
I dreamt of a lion's den and different types of hen.
I dreamt of dragons and knights
especially when they begin to fight.
I dreamt of flowers and enchanted powers
I dreamt of ghouls and little elf fools.
Funny places and pony races.
I saw a giant eagle, I was scared.
I was talking to a chicken in my kitchens.
Is this a dream?
Oh if it is I must be silly!

Emily Reeves (8)
Henleaze Junior School

MY VOYAGE TO A STAR

I made my destiny,
I got right to a star,
I climbed aboard
And started to walk,
But fell off the other side!

Colours passed until I ended,
I slowly drifted
To the Earth and went through the atmosphere.
I'd made my journey come true!

Nicola Rees (10)
Henleaze Junior School

THE MAGIC BOX

I will put in my box
The golden sun shining on the bluest sea reflecting on the sand.

I will put in my box
The lovely smells of a red strawberry-scented candle.

I will put in my box
The biggest, shiny, red and green scale from the tip of a dragon's tail.

I will put in my box
The most fantastic taste of Chinese food in a sea-blue bowl.

I will put in my box
The twinkle of the tiniest star in the huge black sky.

I will put in my box
The sweetest song of the singing nightingale.

My box is made of pure gold,
It has a silver lock and two bronze hinges.

In my box I will swing on the branch of the oldest oak tree in the snow.

Sophie Helena Moody (10)
Henleaze Junior School

THE NIGHT

A crisp, cold, dark sky,
Lit up by little balls of flaming fire,
A frosted, silent wind whistles in my ears,
Birds screeching and squawking like black thunder,
The moon shimmers on the water like shattered crystal.

Edward Benjamin (9)
Henleaze Junior School

I Walked Through The Swaying Roses

I walked through the swaying roses,
Past the dancing daffodils,
And down to the stream,
Which was as wide as an elephant,
As quiet as a church,
And as deep as a thought.
The swans swam gracefully across the dazzling lake,
The sun shone down,
Its rays shining on me as if I were a God.
I headed north and found the sweetest ducklings following their mother,
I wandered around to find a purple box, lying on the ground
      like a brick.
Questioning my thought, I opened it,
Inside lay a red mirror and a blue brush.
I carried on, the box in my pocket, but this time heading east,
To find what I was looking for . . . the tulip field!

Charlotte Seymour (9)
Henleaze Junior School

At The Beach

I was at the beach, listening to the waves crumbling on the sand.
It splashed my toes as I sat happily, listening to the roar of the sea.
The sea was as blue as the sky, as I saw the horizon from where I was.
I trailed my hand in the cold water, as I looked out at sea.
I lay on the sand, humming a tune as I kicked my feet in the waves.
I heard my name called in imagination, as I hummed my tune.
It was a lovely day.

Tamar Nunn (8)
Henleaze Junior School

MY GARDEN

If you take one step into my garden
you will see a sort of vision
If you take four steps more
you will feel like floating in the air
in my beautiful garden of joy and laughter

Swaying bluebells dance in the wind
squirrels jump from branch to branch
the old oak tree soaks its feet in the sleeping stream
which lays nearby

At night the stars look like diamonds in the sky
moonlight pours into my Garden of Eden
you will not want to leave my wondrous garden.

Amy Willerton (8)
Henleaze Junior School

CHATSWORTH WATERFALL

The waterfall rippled down
with its slippery tail following behind
such a wonderful feeling struck my heart.

From top to bottom
oh so high! Oh so low!
From the Scottish mountains to the English Channel
that wonderful sight I saw.

A shower of diamonds
shining like cats' eyes
that paints a picture to last
forever.

Emily Greenslade (9)
Henleaze Junior School

MAJORCA

The beach is a sandy island
full of children
playing and having fun

The sea is a silver ball
full of glass fish, small and large
and boats float away like seagulls resting in the sea

The streets are stretched, long and far
with shops side by side
like eggs wrapped up in their nest

The setting sun is amazing!
A giant, red rose
hovering over Majorca.

Andrew Watts (8)
Henleaze Junior School

THE JUNGLE

In the silent night parrots squawk
Water crashing against rocks
Crocodiles snapping like barking dogs.
The tiger prowling along
Searching for his prey, pounces,
Ripping his prey apart one piece at a time.
Out of nowhere comes the howling,
The silent slithering of the snakes with their slimy bodies
Covered in patterns.
Silence no more
In the jungle!

Lauren Davies (8)
Henleaze Junior School

BRIXHAM

Through the windows
I see a golden rose placed in the morning sky
as if it is held by glue for ever

Downstairs the stone walls are as cold as ice
through the old rooms there is a swing door
cold air swarms in, making the room chilly

Open streets of cobbled lanes
smooth, brown
and worn away

Along the harbour the water laps against the edge
playing with the light in the gleam of the moon.

Lucy Gilbert (10)
Henleaze Junior School

THE DUSTMAN NEXT DOOR

The dustman next door plays the most peaceful instrument
He says it was created by a cascading waterfall
He found it as fresh as a daisy on a river bank
When he plays it, the musician seems to turn into a seabird
Defending its eggs with talons as hard as nails
And wings as black as coal
He calls it
Ogara
When I am in the presence of this music,
I seem to feel the bird itself perching on my shoulder
I love the feeling
And I love the
Dustman next door.

Robert Newman (9)
Henleaze Junior School

THE FANTASTIC PLACE

The gleaming sun shines
night and day
as if he was saying
I don't want to go away
the sun in Cyprus happily stays
over the bays

The majestic waves reach the sky every day
when I'm walking by
reaching up to the stars above
making a show of its diamond glory

The marvellous view just goes up to you
saying, 'Who are you?'
It is a sight to see

My favourite part comes last of all . . .
like a swarm of fireflies
the lights paint a rainbow of colours
as the night goes by.

Sophia Kallias (8)
Henleaze Junior School

MY LITTLE FRUIT TREE

It is as quiet as a hedgehog hibernating
The moonlight is gleaming on it
As beautiful as a sapphire sparkling in delight
My own little fruit tree in the park
Her soft little leaves are dancing in the gentle wind
She looks like a pop star with a lovely smile
She is my little fruit tree glittering away in the moonlight
She is as quite as a hedgehog hibernating.

Zoe Bond (8)
Henleaze Junior School

THE LITTLE WRECK

A little boat set-off from the rocky bays of a sandy beach.
The sea was as calm as the gentle breeze on a cool summer's day.
Slowly the boat started to sway.
The sea was getting rough.
Suddenly . . . the waves crashed,
As though a water musician was playing the aqua cymbals.
The wind howled, like a shaggy wolf yelping from hunger.
The storm blazed on,
As though the Gods of seas and water were angry with the little wreck.
Hand-like waves carried the little wreck to a desert island in the middle
	of nowhere.
Where the crew decided to stay and live forever and ever with the
	little wreck.

Hilary Orchard (11)
Henleaze Junior School

A RIVER IN G MAJOR

Music is water,
Travelling, gushing,
Around the world,
Sometimes only a little trickle,
At others, roaring waterfalls
Ever flowing, ever rippling,
A non-stop melody.
Sprightly, moving noises,
Eerie, immutable sounds.
Water is a music that will never, ever die.

Isobel Booth (11)
Henleaze Junior School

THE COLD WEEK

Monday the ice blizzard comes to us
Tuesday the gloomy, darkening, howling, bitter sky came crowding
 around us
Wednesday the whistling wind comes to school
Thursday the cold, feathery flakes come looming down from the
 icy sky
Friday the moaning, gripping, lashing lightning came with a storm
 of rain
Saturday the looming, growing cloud comes with handfuls of snow
Sunday the bitter, numbing, relentless cold comes
The whole month was like a roaring, horrible, miserable, frightening
 thing.
It was as wet as a swimming pool with a giant lightning storm.

Tara-Louise Seddon (8)
Henleaze Junior School

COMET

It's a gigantic bonfire burning bright,
Crashing to Mars it sets alight.
It's like a bullet just to be shot,
A dented ball of rock.
A fierce red tail trails along,
When it hits it's like a bomb.
An explosion arises into the air,
Pieces of rock are scattered everywhere.
Now the planet has a hole,
Like a football through the goal.

David Cook (11)
Henleaze Junior School

ELEPHANTS

Elephants are large,
Large as can be.
Elephants are large,
As large as a tree.
They stay in groups,
With their mum and dad.
They are sometimes naughty,
Mischievous and bad.
They are very nice,
They are lovely,
They are scared of mice.
Elephants are large,
Large as can be.
Elephants are large,
As large as a tree.

Hope Gallie (10)
Henleaze Junior School

WATERFALL

Glinting, gleaming and sparkling,
As clear as a crystal,
Cascading down the rocks
A vertical drop!
A natural wonder of the world
Glistening, glimmering and flashing,
Bursting with wildlife!

Daniel Kohn (8)
Henleaze Junior School

THE MOON

The moon is brighter
The moon is lighter
All in one colour

The moon is round
And easily found
Whenever you look in the sky

The moon has a face
A graceful face
In space

The moon is brighter
The moon is lighter
All in one colour

Aseel Basson (8)
Henleaze Junior School

WORK

I hate working,
It's boring and tiring,
Ironing, washing up, cooking,
All of them work and boring,
I like to sleep and watch TV,
Better than driving, driving to work,
I go down the street and see my neighbours,
I wave, they wave back to me,
Then it just hits me - why do I go to work?

Alanna Hyde (9)
Henleaze Junior School

The Voyage Of A Raindrop

My cloud drifts slowly through the sky,
Crushed, squashed, no room to move.
We wobble inside, my family and I,
Unsure of what awaits us.
The wind pushes harder against the cloud,
A sparkling light appears below,
Frightened, our silent screams grow loud.
Air rushes past as we fall and scatter,
A sense of fear goes through me,
Spinning around I meet the hungry Earth
Which sucks me in,
I am free to nourish the land and give life.

Emily Adcock (10)
Henleaze Junior School

Time Travel

I'm dizzy and frightened
I'm lost in time
I'm confused and sick
It's like being a child alone in a maze
My time machine has broken
It's flowing in space
What shall I do? I've got no idea
I'm alone and scared in this universe
I'm floating away, away, away
What shall I do?

Catherine Holloway (11)
Henleaze Junior School

LIFE

He's closed inside a place, with veins and nerves,
His head and spine merely curves,
With his mother's heart beating in his ear
Which he will continually hear,
No more is he curled
For now he is in the real world,
Mewling in his mother's arms.
Now an infant speaking the words of life
And walking the steps of life,
Sleeping with a huge world spread around.
School is the next thing.
No longer is it the beginning,
Boredom now strikes
Which no one likes,
And the world is still so large.
Teenage years is another thing,
No longer is it boring.
Love strikes!
He writes messages of love to his mistress,
But she refuses him,
So soon, he has the feeling of sadness,
The world means nothing now.
Adulthood has become,
Now he is just one,
Sat by the fire,
Worn out entire,
The world is even greater than when an infant.
Then to the floor falls he, with only blankness to guide him.

Emily Daly (10)
Henleaze Junior School

GRANDAD

When Grandad died
We wept like gushing rain
I will never leave that feeling
Ever, ever . . .

Realise what it must be like
Grandad was a god of kindness
Only to be tranquil and free

He had a peaceful death
We wept like torrential rain
Me especially!
For he was my God
He was.

Harriet Booth (8)
Henleaze Junior School

TOOTH FAIRY

There was a shout,
'My tooth has fallen out!'
He put it under his pillow that night
and woke to find a shining light.
'Is that a tooth fairy?'

She looked like a plasticine woman
with a mouth of leaves and a cloak of cobwebs
hair of bright light
and fifty pence to my delight!

Michael Cook (8)
Henleaze Junior School

THE WAY TO CALIFORNIA

You walk up the stairs
Take your seat
People crowding on
Your stomach turning upside down
As you leave the ground
You're flying high in the sky
Hostesses are walking around
Clouds fly by your window
As you doze into a dream
The pilot announces, 'Fasten your seat belt
For two weeks of sunshine and glory
'Cos we're *California* bound.'

Vicki Jane Squires (10)
Henleaze Junior School

JOURNEY TO SPACE

Out in space it's a wonderful place,
It's empty, huge and quiet.
There are Martians with bellies which wobble like jellies
To digest their diet.

There's white moon cheese and Saturn peas,
Toasted with Neptune bread.
And sun-baked chips with moon fruit pips
Which they suck when they go to bed.

. . . But I prefer human food to chew,
But that's just me, hey how about you?

David Mark Cordell (10)
Henleaze Junior School

JOURNEY AROUND THE GLOBE

Idly I spin my globe
A round the world journey begins in my head.
I start at Great Britain, a tiny pink dot,
Starting to spin it, where will it stop?
Whizzing past Fiji, Australia too,
Home to koala and great kangaroo.
I spin my globe again,
And find myself in Spain
Where the bulls and the matadors fight,
And guitarists play into the night.
Down to Antarctica,
The freezing South Pole
Where the Earth is threatened by the ozone hole.
Suddenly I stop my globe.
My round the world journey ends in my head.

Luke Steven (9)
Henleaze Junior School

TITANIC

There she goes through the harbour gates,
People cheering, paint gleaming, propellers splashing,
Smoke churning in the air.
The tugs let go and off she goes on her first and last voyage.
She is picking up speed as she towers over the factories
And stone houses of Southampton dock.

Niall Spencer (10)
Henleaze Junior School

FROST

When frost comes sweeping across the land,
Licking, turning each blade of grass,
When the lake is glazed over,
And birds and bees are in their nest
Frost comes riding.

And when it begins to snow,
He will look out on the streets and fields below,
Frost will stop -
His work complete.

But, when he sees a child's smile
As it trudges along the crispy white path,
A corner of his heart breaks
And there he'll lie
'Til winter dies.
His work complete.

Joshua Greenfield (10)
Hillcrest Primary School

WOLF

I stealthily stalk my prey and then pounce on it,
Then I savagely disembowel it,
And greedily rip out bloody organs and muscle,
I feast on its fresh body and slurp up its blood,
I dispose of the mangy body
And wash myself in the eddies and currents of the cold, fast river,
I return to my messy den to wait for my next unlucky meal!

Rory McLoughlin (11)
Hillcrest Primary School

DEAR PENCIL CASE...

Dear pencil case,
Please let me out,
I've got a sore throat,
So I can't really shout,
My lead has gone blunt,
I feel like the runt,
Of the pencils in here,
Oh dear, oh dear!

My paint is all chipped,
My rubber is too,
I feel really embarrassed,
In front of the rest who are new,
So please let me out,
I don't like it in here,
If you set me free,
I'll never shed another tear.

    Yours sincerely

Josie Berry (10)
Hillcrest Primary School

THE CHINCHILLA

I can jump out of my cage
I can leap and hop around
I can fly from my cage
But never can be found

I have got a lovely owner
I have been fed every day
I have got a wonderful owner
But it's good I don't have to pay

I got outside the house once
I got out and about
I got out of the doors once
But I did have my doubts

I like it where I'm living
I like it lots right here
I like it at this lovely home
Because I've never been in fear

Jethro Gilbert (11)
Hillcrest Primary School

THE CRASH

I was walking along behind the back of school,
It was a calm and chilled atmosphere,
It was so still and silent, so silent you could hear a pin drop.

Suddenly the silence was broken by a loud screech,
Followed by an ear-splitting yell,
I panicked and hurried round the corner.

When I got round the corner there was a blue Volvo on top of a boy,
The boy had blood oozing out of his head,
I looked in the car, the driver was out cold.

I panicked,
I was worried,
I ran and ran.

When I got home I told no one,
I regret running away now,
Because he's in the land of the gods.

Jacob Lamb (11)
Hillcrest Primary School

THE BALLOON

I've got a balloon.
I hold the balloon tight because it will fly away.
The balloon is red.
The balloon is quite big.
The string went out of my hand.
The balloon is getting smaller.
My balloon flew away.
The balloon went over the school.
It is very small from the garden.
The rain is coming down so it popped.
'Poor girl!'
I am so sad.
Oh you stupid girl.

Sally Langdon (11)
Hillcrest Primary School

SPECIAL PLACE

Sometimes I like to sit in my special place and dream.
Dream of sandy beaches and the sun shining on a sea of stars.
Everyone laughs there, all of them are happy.
When I wake up I am happy.
So I go on and have another dream.

This dream is I am in the country
And I am on a grass bed.
Butterflies are flying around me
The sun is shining on me.

Now I wake up and feel really happy.
So now I walk out and remember that it is school tomorrow.

Anna Milby (8)
Hillcrest Primary School

POOR PENCIL

Please pencil case,
Please let me out,
I'm dented, bented,
Too much rented.

Please pencil case,
Please let me out,
I'm tired, but still hired,
Wanting to be fired.

Please pencil case,
Please let me out,
I'm scratched, batched,
Okay you've won the match -

But don't expect me to work.

Alice Wyatt (9)
Hillcrest Primary School

CAN ANYONE OUT THERE ...

Can anyone out there help me?
I feel really empty,
I've never been used,
Since I was abused.

I've been treated like dirt,
And it really hurt,
I'm stuck in this dump,
On my head is a lump.
Can anyone out there help me?

Ellena Caudwell (10)
Hillcrest Primary School

THE SUN!

In the summer it blazes down,
In the winter it hibernates.
In summer months,
The sun looks like a crown,
It blazed down on me all day,
And makes me feel all warm and lazy,
Temperature rising from 1-50,
Shining bright up in the sky,
Slowly moving round the world.
Here comes autumn, now it's winter,
The sun is hibernating,
It seems so dark without the sun,
I look out the window, and feel so sad,
Now that the sun has gone.
Oh! When will spring come?
Come back sun,
Please bring back that lovely fun!

Dorothy Thompson (10)
Hillcrest Primary School

ALL THE COLOURS OF THE RAINBOW

Yellow is sunny, bright and cosy.
Green is light and bright and nosy.
Orange is warm, snug and fluorescent.
Purple is dark, sharp, evil like the night.
Red is bright like the Devil in Hell
Jumping and bubbling, burning below the stairs.

Ruby Bell (8)
Hillcrest Primary School

MY BIG, FAT BUNNY

I have a big, fat bunny,
He has a very round tummy,
He goes around all day,
Eating all his hay.

I have a big, fat bunny,
He likes it when it's sunny,
He has lovely white paws,
Which get stuck under our doors.

I have a big, fat bunny,
He is very funny,
When he is happy,
He's a very nice chappy.

And that is my big, fat bunny.

Emily Burke (10)
Hillcrest Primary School

NIGHT VISITOR

Watch out at 12 o'clock
Just in case you tread on me
If you do I will curl up like a spiky golf ball
I am shy, no one's around at midnight
If I hear you I will run away
My twig-like legs won't carry me very fast
I have X-ray eyes so I can see you coming

Alex Youé (10)
Hillcrest Primary School

THE WHITE, WHITE WINTER

It's cold and frosty,
On the window,
Like a picture by an artist.
Freezing nights,
Unlike the summer,
It's nice and cosy,
Wrapped up warm,
With gloves, a scarf, a bobble hat.
Get outside,
White trees,
White cottage,
Snow!
Crisp,
Crack,
Crunch,
Snow!
Red lights, green trees,
But everywhere,
Lots of white.
Why not have a snowball fight?
Called back in,
Everyone's so excited,
It's Christmas Eve,
So Santa's here!

Rebecca Harvey (9)
Hillcrest Primary School

WINTER

Wrap-up warm!
It's ever so cold,
With frost
And snowflakes flying down
Like spider's webs
Hanging from the grey window sill.

Wrap-up warm!
It's ever so cold,
Fairy lights glistening
From the sharp Christmas tree,
Tinsel hanging, crackers banging
Because it's Christmastime.

Wrap-up warm!
It's ever so cold,
I can smell Christmas dinner,
I can feel the warm fire
Getting hotter and hotter
The doorbell rings its carols.

Wrap-up warm!
It's ever so cold,
Decorations hanging
From the pure white ceiling,
Outside snow has settled,
Rested, for another white wintertime.

Emily Nicholas (9)
Hillcrest Primary School

WINTER

Winter is
Cold,
Dark,
Depressing.
Then finally,
Christmas comes.
You'll find the colour that's been waiting,
Deep in your heart.
Trees are draped
With frost and snow,
Children make angels
In the deep, frosty ground,
Then sit by the fire at home.
Then, next day,
The snowmen are dead,
The ice on the ground has vanished,
Squirrels wake from hibernation,
It's *spring!*

Lucy Stephens (10)
Hillcrest Primary School

HOMELESS AND HUNGRY

I'm lying there -
In my cardboard bed,
With the sound of thunder
Like a glass breaking outside.
I crawl out of my cardboard bed,
To find food.

I'm out and find a piece of bread
Burnt like blackened wood,
But it looks lovely.
I eat it happily.

I hear that noise - is it thunder again?
It's getting louder, louder, louder.
Bombs!
The sky lights up - like it was firework night.

Harry Byrne (9)
Hillcrest Primary School

WINTERTIME

Winter comes,
Things freeze again
Branches stand bare -
Like bony fingers.
Ponds freeze up,
Icy and cold.
You've been warned, you've been told
About winter
When snowflakes fall
And sometimes settle on your wall.

Winter can be nice, it can be jolly,
Winter brings - lots of holly.
It brings Christmas, a lovely time,
A time to share -
(Don't leave Christmas trees bare!)

Christmas is a happy time,
With carols and presents,
But wrap up warm,
Or stay inside,
Read a book by the fire,
Or just do what is *your* desire.

Anna Barlow (10)
Hillcrest Primary School

THE NIGHT I MADE AN ODDVAR!

On Monday evening, after school,
My father said to me;
'I've got a job that's really cool,
Why don't you come and see?'

He tipped a box out on the floor
And there before my eyes -
A pile of wood and screws fell out,
'It's an *Oddvar*,' he replies.

With Allen key and screwdriver,
We followed every rule,
We fitted it together -
The bits became a stool.

Oddvar is just its name,
Its use is very clear,
Our guests can have it by their bed,
So that their lamp is near.

Jess Roome (11)
Hillcrest Primary School

DOLPHIN

Water passes my smooth, cool body as I swim through the sea,
I quickly rush away from my predators as fast as I can,
My lovely skin hides me in the sea.

All I want to do is play all day with my friends,
I really am a happy fella,
I love playing around with my friends.

Elizabeth Studley (10)
Hillcrest Primary School

THE UNSTOPPABLE PIG

It charged straight through Trafalgar Square,
and pinched somebody's underwear.
It dumped some dung in the park,
then a big dog saw it and started to bark.
It barged straight into somebody's house,
then came out the back whilst eating a mouse.
They called up the army to kill the strange pig,
but it went straight through disguised as a wig.
They soon realised and started to shoot,
it ran up a chimney and came out in soot.
It ran into a bank and started to kill,
everyone called it Mr Piggy Bill.

Joseph Bowles (11)
Hillcrest Primary School

DRAGONS

His red eyes glow - like burning coal,
Sleeps in a cave - without a soul.

A flaming oven in each lung,
Not forgetting the forked fireproof tongue.

When a dragon breathes its breath -
Everything turns to death.

Tired, hungry but still wants flesh,
He wants it human -
Young
And
Fresh.

Theo Bond (10)
Hillcrest Primary School

WINTERTIME

What do you *see* in the frozen lake?
It's winter.
Can you *hear* it,
Brushing against the trees.
It's winter.
Can you *feel* the snow?
It's very cold and white,
That's what winter's like.
The trees are bare,
And sometimes bushes,
Reaching out and *touching*,
Winter.
The ground is frosty,
The sky is grey,
But, because it's Christmas
People shout
Wahay!

Omar Ali (10)
Hillcrest Primary School

RATTLESNAKE

Fangs - like twin swords.
Tail like a baby's rattle.
Scales like diamonds -
Eyes like coal-studded emeralds.
A limbless body like a mop
Slithers around like a crocodile in water.

Alex Rose (9)
Hillcrest Primary School

THE WINTER BIRD

She swoops down,
Like a falling leaf,
Onto the icy, wet snow.
Then back into the sky she soars,
But, something is wrong,
A beating sound from behind,
Sounding like two rulers,
Being snapped together.
Then,
Bang!
She falls, falls,
Falls onto the icy, wet snow.
But the injured bird gets back up again
And carries on peacefully,
With her life in the sky.

Caroline Sinclair (9)
Hillcrest Primary School

HAMSTER

It nibbles
A snug cuddler
A nocturnal animal
Long fur
Very small
Nose twitcher
Furiously fast
A fur ball
A digger

Zoe Brock (10)
Longwell Green Primary School

TIGER

A loud noise maker,
A fast runner,
A furry striped animal,
A paw print maker,
A fierce mammal,
A big biter,
A sun relaxer,
A hungry hunter,
A fluffy-faced menace,
A bone cruncher,
A spiked teeth-eater,
A quiet walker,
A pouncing jumper,
A tail swinger,
A claw trimmer.

Katie Manfield (11)
Longwell Green Primary School

OWL

A night flyer
An ear nipper
A letter carrier
A soft hooter
A skilled hunter
A feathered friend
A stealth glider
A mouse eater

Christopher Miller (11)
Longwell Green Primary School

THE DARK

It's dark and gloomy,
It's pitch black,
It's cold and freezing.

The worst part about it,
Is the stillness,
The black, black stillness.

The wind is whistling,
The twigs are scraping,
The doors are rattling.

I shivered with fright,
As shadows crept over,
The wall.

Abigail McCarthy (10)
Longwell Green Primary School

GETTING LOST IN DEBENHAMS

Getting lost in Debenhams is such a fun thing.
Up and down the escalators, your family wondering.
Going to the toy shop, playing with the toys,
Sitting in the corner making lots of noise.
Getting bored with the toys, want to try the perfume.
Going to the perfume shop, such a funny thing,
Squirting all the perfume, everybody coughing.
Mum and dad find you, lots of bills to pay.
You get ready to

Run away!

Richard James & Mike Cox (11)
Longwell Green Primary School

BUNNY RABBIT

A foot thumper,
A fur ball,
A small bouncer,
A big hearer,
A veg cruncher,
A tall springer,
A powder puff,
A fluffy creature,
A high hopper,
A grass muncher,
A fur coat,
A cotton tail,
A hay sucker,
A nose twitcher.

Becky Garland (10)
Longwell Green Primary School

I'M MUCH BETTER THAN YOU

I have longer hair than you,
I go to ballet too,
I can stand on my tiptoes.

    I'm just so much better than you.

I have higher heels than you,
I go to gymnastics too,
I can do flips and the splits

    I'm just so much better than you.

Leah Saunders (10) & Charlotte Smith (11)
Longwell Green Primary School

THE WHITE TIGER

Its nose is like a ripe raspberry in the summer
And whiskers like bristles on an old man's chin.

Ears like badgers' paws,
A beauty contest this tiger is sure to win.
Eyes like sparkling black pearls,
Its body is like lots of black swirls.
Velvety fur stripes, so soft and black.
Shhh! While he's sleeping or he will awake
And
You'll get a
   Smack!

Stephanie Youmans (9)
Longwell Green Primary School

THE WHITE TIGER

It creeps down to search for food
When it is close enough
It will go for it.
It has four legs and runs very fast.
It lives in snow.
His nose looks like a T
And he has big feet.
His whiskers are like string
And teeth are like vampire teeth.
He is very big
And his skin is like a rug.

Ryan Cleaves (10)
Longwell Green Primary School

The Lion

A face like a fierce bear.
A mane like a pretty pink tutu.
Teeth like sharp daggers.
Eyes like huge raisins.
A leather moist nose.
Stalks pray in the undergrowth.

Rebecca Dimes (9)
Longwell Green Primary School

The Shark

The shark moves stealthily like a submarine
Fin swishing side to side
The shark is the killer of the sea
Some people end up inside.

Teeth like sharp razors
It's a man-eating machine
When there's sharks around
The water isn't very clean.

James Clover (9)
Longwell Green Primary School

The Kitten

Fur is like clouds
Small little pink tongue
Whiskers like frosty grass
Eyes like green grapes
Nose as white as snow

Jenny Selman (10)
Longwell Green Primary School

THE SQUIRREL

The squirrel is big
And the tail's like a fluffy ball
And he eats nuts and berries
He is a good jumper
And he eats cones.

Rachel Seel (10)
Longwell Green Primary School

THE DEER

Antlers like a Viking's hat
Looks like white paint had been flicked on it
Prickly like an orange door mat
Nose like a lump of coal

Antlers grow each year
Eyes like black marbles
Black and white rear
White stick legs.

Claire Uppington (9)
Longwell Green Primary School

THE HORSE

Hooves like a clomping machine
Galloping through the meadow,
Mane like a big sheet of paper
Blowing in the wind,
Neighs like a passing train.

Hayley Benjamin (10)
Longwell Green Primary School

CRASH, BANG

Crash!
Bang!
The iron man landed with a *clang!*

He stamped his foot on the ground
Ran around until he was found.

The farmers were furious!
Said, *'That's it!'*
Then they put him in a pit.

A *big black dragon* was seen in the stars
All the astronomers said, 'He's from Mars.'

The dragon landed on the mountains with a *crash!*
So all the mountaineers got turned into *mash*.

Michael Stinson (8)
Longwell Green Primary School

THE SHARK

The shark is . . .

A sneaky hunter,
With razor-sharp teeth
And a terrifying fin.
A vicious carnivore,
Moving like a bullet,
And snapping up meat
Like a sleek silver whale.
The shark is the gangster of the sea.

Andrew Selman (10)
Longwell Green Primary School

THE HORSE

A horse gallops up and down,
Like brainwaves upon the shore,
As it stamples on the waving grass,
It kills part of living nature.

And the gentle breeze picked up,
The horse's spiky mane,
And dropped it again,
As the breeze left.

The horse crunched on the sweet grass,
Having a nice evening meal,
And as it lies down for a rest,
The world is at peace.

Beth Doyle (10)
Longwell Green Primary School

THE MANTA RAY

The manta ray
Is very flat,
Swimming towards the bay,
The manta ray looks like a bat,
Swimming towards the shore.

The manta ray
Has a tail pointed like a nail,
Swimming towards the bay,
Watching the people sail,
Swimming towards the shore.

Daniel Whybrew (10)
Longwell Green Primary School

THE BIG THING

I saw it . . . Hmmm let me think . . . *there!*
    I was running!
I turned to see his eyes
    They were like headlamps
Glowing bright red.
    Then I noticed his body.
It was as big as a *house!*
    Did you hear his feet?
They were as big as a bed!
    They went *Stomp! Stomp! Stomp!*
There was a dent in his head.
    It was a *big* one!
Did you see it?
    I did!

Sophie Worsfold (8)
Longwell Green Primary School

THE SNOW

I like the snow
It should come every year
I like to smear the soft white snow
Off the ground
I pound the snow
Into fluffy white balls
And at night
I hear the snowman call.
As the snow fades away
I wipe a tear off my face

David Cardy (9)
Longwell Green Primary School

THE IRON MAN'S BODY PARTS

The iron man's fingers are like a computer keyboard
But there are no keys!
The iron man's body is as strong as 3000 men and women
But his fingers are not!
The iron man's feet are as big as two houses put together
But his toes aren't.
The iron man is as big as a terribly tall tree!
The iron man's eyes are as big as a computer
But the screen does not come on!
The iron man's ears are as big as a chair
But nobody sits on it!
The iron man's head is like a dustbin
But nobody throws trash in it!
The iron man's arms are like two elephants' trunks
But they do not squirt water!

Michael Thomas (8)
Longwell Green Primary School

THE BOBCAT

His nose like a tiny little cherry
Ears like a hair clip
Paws that hang off rocks
Dots where his whiskers are
Like chicken pox
Markings around his face
That go into his eyes
Whiskers that poke out
That bend at the end.

Becki Keen (10)
Longwell Green Primary School

The Lions

The lion lies on the rock with her mate
Eyes on the lookout at all times
Ears pricked up like a dark open cave
Nose like a mouse's face with no fur
Fur as golden as the sun
Their whiskers can tickle you a lot

Georgina Dann (10)
Longwell Green Primary School

The Hamster

Its skin is furry
It's as round as a ball
Its eyes are like raisins
Its nose is so pink
It moves like a mouse
Its ears are like peanuts

Joshua Willis (0)
Longwell Green Primary School

The Cygnet

It waddles like a toddler
It's like a fluffy snowball
With a pointed stone for a beak
Shy, black, pearl eyes
And little, flat, webbed feet.

Emma Youmans (9)
Longwell Green Primary School

THE BODY OF THE IRON MAN

His body is as big as a house.
The head is as big as a dustbin.
He has light eyes and a massive mouth.
His feet are as smelly as cheese!
His ears are smaller than an ant.
His arms are strong and marvellous.
The nose is a pig's nose . . .

Simon Lewis (8)
Longwell Green Primary School

THE ELEPHANT

Tusks like spears,
Bats wings for ears.
Big, heavy feet,
Eats no meat.
Tail like a window wiper,
Not as deadly as the Viper.

Lewis Toghill (9)
Longwell Green Primary School

THE PEACOCK BUTTERFLY

It flies freely in the morning sky
Its spots are like eyes
Flowers are food, antennae on top
That's the Peacock Butterfly.

James Dix (10)
Longwell Green Primary School

THE IRON MAN

The iron man is as tall as a block of flats.
He is as heavy as a house.
His eyes are as colourful as a rainbow!
His body is as big as two tables put together!
He has a nose as long as a pencil.

Lucy Davis (8)
Longwell Green Primary School

THE GUINEA PIG

There it is
Lying in the hay
Fur like a sheep
Nose like a sweet
Eyes like pebbles
Noise like a car engine
Ears like hamster hair
Feet like a rat
Silver, my guinea pig.

Alice Drury Webb (9)
Longwell Green Primary School

THE BLACK PANTHER

His eyes are like lights in the distance
And his fur like a black rug
He catches his food and gets what he wants
The king of the jungle
He is! He is!

Liam Jacques (9)
Longwell Green Primary School

THE IRON MAN!

The iron man's arms are like fishing rods.
The iron man's eyes are like lamps.
The iron man's legs are like lamp posts.
His body is like a boulder.
His hair is like spaghetti.

Jack Denning (8)
Longwell Green Primary School

THE FOX

His eyes are like beads.
He is as thin as a rake.
His ears are like a telephone hook.
His nose is a black marble.
He snaps like scissors.
His tail's a brush.
His legs are twigs.
He's very sly like a detective.
But his fur's as cuddly as a teddy!

Alex Ash (10)
Longwell Green Primary School

THE HORSE

Mane like sheets of paper blowing in the wind,
Tail like a feather duster,
Eyes like beautiful marbles,
Body that gleams like silk,
Hooves clatter like nuts and bolts.

Leanne Pople (9)
Longwell Green Primary School

THE IRON MAN

The iron man's head is as big as a bin
He is very strong so he will always win.

He likes eating bread
But he loves chocolate spread.

His eyes are as round as a tennis ball
He can step over every wall!

He hates reading a book
But he will have a good look.

He came down from the sky
But he never learned to fly!

Grace Lewis (8)
Longwell Green Primary School

THE SPACE BAT ANGEL DRAGON

The space bat angel dragon is so big.
It has black eyes and when they move
They go ping, ping.

Clonk went the tail when it hit the ground.
The body is as heavy as 100 elephants on top of each other.

The size of it covers the whole of Australia.

Smash went the space bat angel dragon when it hit Australia.

The space bat angel dragon's face went *clang* when it hit the floor.

Edward Downing (8)
Longwell Green Primary School

THE IRON MAN

The iron man is 100 feet high!
He is stronger than an elephant!
His favourite food is metal!
He's made out of iron!
His head is as big as a bin
With arms like a tree trunk,
With legs like roads,
With a huge body,
With eyes that shine out,
With ears like broken plates,
With a nose like cardboard,
With a mouth like a banana,
With hair like pigtails that curl
And feet like pineapples.
He is huge!

Emma Alway (8)
Longwell Green Primary School

THE IRON MAN!

The iron man is as *big* as a tree.
His eyes are as *bright* as a lamp.
He has a head as *strong* as a car.
His ears are as small as a slippery fish.
He has hair as *swirly* as spaghetti.
The iron man's body is as *hard* as a house.
His arms are as *long* as a tree trunk.
He has legs as *heavy* as a computer.
The iron man's feet are as *smelly* as a dustbin.

Josie Smith (8)
Longwell Green Primary School

ANIMALS

There was a lonely frog
That sat on its very own log.
There is a lion that is scared of the light
Because he has had a very big fright.

There was a zebra that was black and white
And it was such a sight.
There was a rabbit
That had such a habit.

One day an animal came over to me
And it was a flea.
A woolly sheep
Was fast asleep.

There was a cat
Chasing a rat.
A tiny mouse
Will buy a house.

Stephanie Cox (9)
Longwell Green Primary School

THE IRON MAN, HOW HE CAME

The iron man came from a country.
He flew a very, very long way.
He came down with a big, big, big *crash!*
The iron man banged his head on the beach - *ouch!*
He got up so fast that he made the world shake.
Then the iron man walked through a wood
To find some metal and a friend.

Lauren Mitchell (8)
Longwell Green Primary School

THE IRON MAN

The iron man is big and strong.
His hair is like spaghetti.
His head is as long as a dustbin.
His ears are as big as books.
His feet are as big as desks.
His body's as long as a classroom.
His arms are as big as two doors.
His legs are as long as three tables.
His eyes are as bright as light bulbs.
His mouth is as wide as a cupboard.
His fingers are as long as two pencils.
His toes are as long as a bookmark.

And the iron man is huge!

Andrew Smith (8)
Longwell Green Primary School

IRON MAN POEM

The iron man is *big* and *heavy*.

His body is made out of iron.
He *storms* about eating metal.

People don't know where he came from.

He's got a loud voice which is very deep.
He is about 20 feet tall.
His eyes light up when he says a few words.

Some people are *scared*, but some are not.

Chelsie Galdies (8)
Longwell Green Primary School

WILL YOU BELIEVE ME?

The iron man's head is as big as a bed!
It is metal and grey and very scary!
His arm is about a yard long!
His body is *huge!*
His legs are so big you should have seen them!
His feet are like cars!
He has eyes that light up!
He has a nose like a chimney!
His ears are like semi-circles!
His mouth is like a banana!
Could someone believe me?
He really is true!

Abigail Allen (9)
Longwell Green Primary School

THE IRON MAN

The iron man's body is as heavy as three elephants!
His arms are as strong as six lions.
His hair is as thin as a piece of string!
His head is as big as a bed.

His mouth is as wide as a classroom!
And as tall as a church.
His eyes glow like a torch.
The iron man's fingers are as big as a pencil
And as knobbly as a doorknob.

Bradley Cox (9)
Longwell Green Primary School

POETIC JOURNEY THROUGH THE MOUTH

In through the mouth, down through the tube.
Acid-type stomach all burning and blue,
Long stringy thing, small intestine, maybe!
When out there I plop,
Fall down a drop.
Even bigger it seems
Large intestine (I dream)
Then without whizzing through, I'm there
Down the loo!
I'll do it again I say!
The person replies, 'No way!'

Claire Moon (11)
Longwell Green Primary School

THE FIGHT

The iron man got on the bed.
The flames were red and hot!
He changed from grey to black to red to white!
Then he got off the bed and shouted to the dragon,
'You have to fly to the sun until you get white hot.'

So the space bat angel dragon flew to the sun until he got white hot.
This time the space bat angel dragon landed.
It was more powerful than last time.

Crash!

Tommy Cains (8)
Longwell Green Primary School

The Weather

When the weather is sunny
I go to the beach to spend my money.
When the weather is bright
The clouds are always white.

When the weather is stormy
I have to take in my laundry.
When the weather is loud
There becomes a great big cloud.

When the weather is rainy
My clothes get all stainy.
When the weather is spitting
My mum does all the knitting.

When the weather is clear
I listen to the radio with my ear.

Sophie Bignell (9)
Longwell Green Primary School

The Iron Man's Body Parts

The iron man's eyes are as bright as headlamps.
His ears are like a dustbin.
His head is as round as a ball
And his mouth is as long as a lamp post!

The iron man's body is as wide as a classroom.
His arms are as long as three tables.
His fingers are as long as five pencils.
His fingernails are as wide as a car!

The iron man's legs are as long as a tree.
His feet are as sharp as a knife.
His toes are as wide as a lunch box
And his toenails are as big as a pocket book!

Samuel Bray (8)
Longwell Green Primary School

THE MONTHS

January is so fun but other times it can be glum.
February can be so cold, other times it can be bold.

The wind in March can be so loud
There's hundreds, lots of smoky clouds.
April brings flowers, mostly all sweet
We always walk by them with our clumsy feet.

May brings lambs while beavers build their dams.
June is sunny, people laugh because some others are being funny.

July is sunny still, the warmth has just opened a new daffodil.
August is when the leaves start to fall,
The wind is draughty, it's trying to call.

Warm September gives the food, other people can be rude.
October brings the pheasant, then to gather nuts is pleasant.

In November the leaves whirl past
And so it brings the windy blast.
December brings the sleet,
Christmas brings all the treats.

Chloé Nowell (8)
Longwell Green Primary School

HOME

I wish I was rich
Because my mum would like to be a witch.
My back garden is really a football pitch,
Even if my brother got chips.

I fiddle with paper clips,
My cousin always has nits.
I run into a pit,
And I'm trying to keep fit.

My dad's name is Bim,
He is very, very dim.
He likes to sing a hymn,
My dog is very thin.

Every time I play on 'Crash Team Racing',
My dog is pacing.
My dog's name is Flick,
And I used to play for Wick.

Matthew Oliver (9)
Longwell Green Primary School

SCHOOL

School is sometimes boring
Even though we're snoring.
The teachers wake us up
And then we grab some cups.

When we are doing maths
We're walking on the paths.
Then we do some literacy
But we're playing with the cutlery.

When I have school dinners
The football team are winners.
Then I go outside
Everyone goes to hide.

Then we do some science
And we learn about an appliance.
At last it's time to go home
So we can dive into foam.

Stephen Walter (9)
Longwell Green Primary School

ANIMAL POEMS

One day my cat
Was sat on a mat
He saw a rat
And down came a hat.

I have a dog
Called Tod
He likes a cup of tea
And he always eats his flea.

I have a mouse called Sherbert
Who has a friend called Herbert.
He is always a good boy
And has a favourite toy.

I once saw a frog
Who was sat on a log.
He went to Spain
And flew in a plane.

April Oxenham (9)
Longwell Green Primary School

MYSELF

There's a hum in the air
But I don't care.
I like you
So give me a clue.

It is so hot
So put it in a pot
With a dot
In a cot.

School is boring
We are snoring.
Teachers wake us up
And give us a cup.

So do a prance
And do it in France.
Then do a dance
In a trance.

Thomas Francis (8)
Longwell Green Primary School

ANIMALS AND PETS

My cat once sat on a mat,
And had an accident with a hat,
The hat was round,
So it made a sound.

I saw a frog who was called Trog,
It sat on a bumpy log,
Along came a frog called Bog,
Who sat on a lumpy log.

My sheep is always asleep,
It doesn't have time to leap,
He is so very puffy,
It makes him look all fluffy.

I had a pet who was a fish,
Who was the size of a very large dish,
I put him in a bowl of water,
And then she gave birth to a daughter.

Rebecca Dale (8)
Longwell Green Primary School

FOOD

My name is Alex Hayes
And I hate mayonnaise
I like ice cream
But I can't user hyper beam

I like hot dog
But I don't have a pet hog
I like to eat peas
But I can't swim the seven seas

I hate cheese
And I hate to be stung by bees
I like chips
They make me top of tips

I like to eat spaghetti
But I can't eat it on the settee
I like ham
But my name isn't Sam.

Alex Hayes (8)
Longwell Green Primary School

THE WORST FAMILY HOLIDAY EVER!

One day we went to Spain
On this huge, lush plane
It was really fun
But the baby was always crying for Mum.

We arrived at Spain
But my brother fell over and was crying with pain
We got to the hotel
And found lots of mail.

We went to the museum
But my big sister was moaning for some silly reason
We watched a show
My favourite character was Mo.

On the way home
My brother wanted to visit the Dome
I said, 'It's not here,'
Then my dad spilt all his beer!

Melanie Williamson (9)
Longwell Green Primary School

A POEM ABOUT ME

My name is Alex Martin
And I like go-karting,
I like reading,
But I hate bleeding.

I'm not foreign,
And I'm not called Lauren.
I'm not from Greece,
But I'm warm in a fleece.

I want a pet snake,
And I like eating cake.
I'm not from France,
And I don't like to dance.

I'm not from Spain,
But my sister's a pain.
I want a pet rat,
And I want him nice and fat.

Alex Martin (8)
Longwell Green Primary School

MY FRIENDS

I've got a friend called Grace,
Who always comes to do a race,
She runs at her fastest pace,
And always comes in first place.

I've got a friend called April Oxenham,
Who eats her toast with jam,
And likes to stroke a little lamb
And likes to eat some ham.

I've got a best friend called Sophie Bignell
And when she sees me she shows a signal.
She has got brown hair
And sits on a brown chair.

I've got a friend called Victoria Downes
And she wears a lot of gowns
And she sometimes frowns
And her hair is brown.

Louise Hendy (9)
Longwell Green Primary School

THE IRON MAN

The iron man can crunch six double-decker buses at the same time.
He makes a noise like 42 elephants.
His head is as big as a dustbin
And if he falls over the world would shake.

The iron man can crunch 1000 classrooms at the same time.
He is as strong as 100 lions.
His eyes glow like the sun.
He can lift up the space bat angel dragon 10 times!

His eyes are as light as 64 light bulbs.
He is as tall as a giraffe!

Tom Churches (8)
Longwell Green Primary School

THE IRON MAN'S HEAD

The iron man's head is as big as a dustbin.
He's made out of invincible iron
In other words - non-breakable.
His eyes are as black as a midnight sky.
His eyes are as long as pencil pots.
His ears are as big as a printer.
His mouth is as big as a table.

The iron man is a monster.

Joe Stansfield (8)
Longwell Green Primary School

MY HOLIDAY

My holiday was hot,
My holiday was fun,
My holiday was playful,
My holiday was very busy.

My holiday was very noisy,
My holiday was excellent,
My holiday was friendly,
My holiday was very crowded.

Claire Case (10)
Luckwell Primary School

SWEETS

S   weets are yummy
W hen they go down my tummy
E   very sweet tastes luscious
E   at, eat, eat, sweets yummy
T   hey are the best
S   weets are the best treats in the world

Marcus Guldbert-Allen (8)
Luckwell Primary School

THE MUCKY MAD MUD MONSTER

The mucky mad mud monster
Is a very nice friend.
But sometimes that can
Come to an end
Because he squashed our windowpane.
Once he went in a bit of a grump
Because he doesn't like a hump.
I like mucky mad mud monster
Because he laughs like me.
He's funny even when he climbs a tree.
The thing I like the best about him
Is that he's my friend.

Lewis Gilbert (7)
Luckwell Primary School

THE DECORATION

A bauble is red.
A bauble is shiny and gold.
A bauble is round.
A bauble is very pretty.
A bauble is very golden.
A Christmas tree is very furry.
A Christmas tree has pretty lights.
A Christmas tree has decorations.
A Christmas tree is green and bushy.
A bauble hangs on a Christmas tree.
A present is under a Christmas tree
Waiting for you
To open it!

Ben Collett (9)
Luckwell Primary School

THE ROLLER COASTER

Faster and faster as it goes
'Weeee!' shout the children
'Ahhhhhh!' shout the mums and dads
As they go faster than ever
It feels dizzy when you go round and round
I can see a drop - ahhhhh!
I can see the grass below, I am very high up
I am scared, I feel like I am going to fall
I feel sick, I am upside down
When I get off I am all over the place
I want to go to bed

Michael Bawn (7)
Luckwell Primary School

ANIMALS

Animals, animals
Horses and hares
Tigers, tigers
Tigers and bears
Parrots, pond skaters
Anacondas and alligators
Hamsters, hogs
Cats and dogs
Jellyfish, jaguars
Dragons and dinosaurs
Tadpoles, terrapins
Monkeys and mice
Baboons, bats
Rabbits and rats
Animals, animals
Animals are great.

Kerry Coles (11)
Luckwell Primary School

IN THE NIGHT

In the night there are owls hooting
In the night there are dogs barking
In the night there are cats purring
In the night there are bats clicking
In the night are hedgehogs creeping
In the night there are foxes running in and out of the bushes
In the night you can hear
Ghosts!

Charlotte Overy (7)
Luckwell Primary School

THE DINOSAUR

The dinosaur is strong
The dinosaur is hungry
The dinosaur is fat
The dinosaur is muscly
The dinosaur is big
The dinosaur is greedy
The dinosaur is green
The dinosaur is scary
The dinosaur is sharp
The dinosaur is smelly
The dinosaur is fierce
The dinosaur is nasty
The dinosaur is vicious.

Bedtime ni-night
My pet dinosaur.

Matthew Hellier (7)
Luckwell Primary School

AT THE BEACH

At the beach there are babies being naughty,
At the beach there are people swimming in the sea,
At the beach there are people queuing for ice cream,
It is nice and really cool but the sun melts it,
At the beach people are playing ball,
There goes the ball, it is going to the sea,
'Stop that ball,' they shout!
At the beach there are babies in the sea with their mums
Teaching their children to swim.

Katie Burge (8)
Luckwell Primary School

COURTNEY

Courtney is my best friend,
He is nice to me,
He is a very great friend to me,
Always wants to be with me.

He is quiet when he plays the PlayStation,
He is very good on the PlayStation,
He lets me in his house,
His house is great.

He is very funny if he comes round
Or I go round his,
He is very fast, nearly the fastest in the class,
He is very strong,
And brilliant at football.

George Cox (10)
Luckwell Primary School

THE SWING

The swing goes high
The swing goes low
The swing wobbles when the wind goes low
In the night the swing is lonely
When it's morning the swing is fun
When it's raining the swing is cold
When it's sunny the swing is funny
When there's a rainbow the swing looks up
When it's snowing the swing is white.

Sophie Jenkins (7)
Luckwell Primary School

AMERICA

Go on red and white Virgin plane,
It's got a small Nintendo screen.
Pick up shining white car,
Go to massive café.

Go to enormous boat safari,
On fast, dark Space Mountain.
Wet by big impact,
On speedy runaway train.

Got all characters' autographs
Tasty chicken nuggets for my tea.
Into room, adjoining doors,
Phew, I'm tired, into bed!

Dale Bright (9)
Luckwell Primary School

THE MOLE WHO LIVES IN THE COMPUTER

The mole who lives in the computer
Is always trying to get out
He tiptoes really quietly inside the keyboard
He always rolls around when no one is about
Mole hides inside the keyboard
When the power is switched on
You'll never ever see him
Has he gone?

Jordan Marsh (7)
Luckwell Primary School

THE CREEPY HOUSE

One night there lived a widow who was sleeping
She was woken up by a noise
She looked in the bathroom
She didn't see anything
When she turned her back she heard a voice
The voice said, 'Whoooo!'
She went downstairs and looked in the kitchen
She saw a shoe
She picked it up
Then she went into the living room
There was a dead man
She called the ambulance.

Paul Rhodes (8)
Luckwell Primary School

ANIMALS

An animal is an okapi with its long, black tongue.
An animal is a capybara, the biggest rodent.
An animal is a tapir with a very long nose.
An animal is a vine snake, an extremely slender one.
An animal is a cougar, a big meat eater.
An animal is a lion with very sharp claws.
An animal is a zebra with black and white stripes.
An animal is a pet like a horse, dog or mouse.
But you've got to be quick
They are coming through the door.
Eeek! Bye!

Lauren Stone (7)
Luckwell Primary School

A Fun Day Out

Wow!
I'm having fun
This ride is cool
It's like Nemesis
I've been on
The merry-go-round
I rode on the horse
I went up and down
Round and round
On the carousel
I screamed
I covered my eyes
Ghosts, vampires, mummies
Came out
And tried to catch us
On the ghost train
Wow!
I'm having fun
I wish this day would never end

Chelsea Emma Harris (10)
Luckwell Primary School

The Stars

The stars are light and bright
They come out at night
They make me fall to sleep
When my mum comes up the stairs
I peep, my eye's half open then I fall to sleep.

Katie Townsend (7)
Luckwell Primary School

NEW YEAR

New Year is a time to enjoy and celebrate
It's a time of hope and colour
Party poppers exploding at midnight
Singing, dancing on the dance floor
Everyone going crazy with streamers and champagne
Everyone desperate to get into the Dome before it turns into nothing
Colourful bursting fireworks
Fizzy drinks flying in the air
The DJ's hat is almost coming off
Because of the music
2001!
Everyone shouts when the clock strikes midnight
A balloon popped
Everyone froze
By the time it took everyone to unfreeze
It was the end of the groovy time
Everyone sighed and went home

    Sweet dreams everyone

Lauren Fay Stuckes (8)
Luckwell Primary School

SNAKES

Snakes are really slimy, slithery.
If you are not careful they will poison you!
They go faster than you, can say boo
Because they have no legs!
The sly snake slides through the sand!

George Tom Smith (8)
Luckwell Primary School

SEASIDE

In and out go the waves.
People sunbathe on the beach.
Children swimming in the sea, splashing in the sea.
In and out go the waves.
In and out go the people eating ice creams.
The sun beats down on the sea and the Punch and Judy.
Lovely smelling doughnuts and fish and chips.
Dead jellyfish and small crabs.
Little fish swimming past your tiny toes.
People screaming and shouting.
People playing beach ball and football.
People smiling.
The beautiful seaside.

James Trenchard (10)
Luckwell Primary School

THE WATERFALL

In a sandy land
There was a waterfall
That stood very tall.
The waterfall reflected,
The waterfall glinted
And danced around in the air.
The waterfall was glittery.
The waterfall was sparkly.
The waterfall was like glass
Shining in the sunlight.

Amy March (8)
Luckwell Primary School

School

I'm in my school I want to get out,
I just would like to shout! Shout! Shout!
I can't wait to see my dad
If I don't I will go mad.

I'm in my school I've changed my mind,
My school teacher is very kind
I read to her nearly every day
I just wish that it could stay that way!

I'm in my school I have to go
My dad says, 'Come on,' - I say, *'No!'*
I'm not in school bye, bye, bye, bye!
I burst out with tears and I cry, cry, cry!

Jemma Hicks (8)
Luckwell Primary School

Volcano

Volcano rocks destroying the town
The scalding hot lava waiting to kill
A big lava monster leaving the town breathless
Then another one *hot, hot, hot!*
A volcano here, a volcano there, what can I do?
Now I'm surrounded, oh dear, oh dear.
I'm running, I'm running, what will happen?
Next a bang, bang, bang!
That's what happened next . . .

Elliot Smith (8)
Luckwell Primary School

ANGUS THE HAMSTER

Angus is my pet hamster.
He is golden with a white, smooth, fluffy belly.
He is fast and speedy.
Angus gnaws on a piece of hard, fruity wood.
He eats his tasty, crunchy hamster food.
He is very cuddly.
Angus is extremely playful.
He runs around his spinning wheel.
When the night is over he lies on his cotton wool
And goes to sleep in dreamland.

    Sweet dreams Angus!

Hannah Milkins (8)
Luckwell Primary School

SLINKING TIGER

Tiger, tiger as light as a feather
Seeks his prey in the dead of the night.
He creeps slowly round the jungle.
On his prowl along comes a hunter
So the tiger hides in the long, long grass.
The hunter walks past.
On its journey the tiger finds a herd of antelope
So he sneaks up to the herd,
Starts to walk faster and faster and faster
Until he grabs and he bites until it falls!
Falls in the grass for the tiger and its cubs to enjoy!

Oliver Chalkley-Brown (8)
Luckwell Primary School

WINTER HOLIDAYS

Got a new snowboard
Chucked a few snowballs
A thick woolly jumper
The hill's a mile long
Big and small jumps
When you land you get a big bump
Hot and cold weather
Fresh pine trees
Snowing all day and night
Houses made out of pine
Clear glass windows
No satellite or cable
Bears outside at night

Tom Delaney (10)
Luckwell Primary School

FOOD

I love the thought of yummy, scrummy food.
Lots of lovely creamy bars of chocolate
And runny chocolate chip ice cream
That melts the minute you put it on your tongue.
Lots of pizza, beans and chips and Angel Delight.
Lots of Cadbury's Cream Eggs with creamy fillings.
You see people walking home with chocolate.
Lots of browny-white bars.
You see the chocolate factory just ahead
And you smell the chocolate being made.
In the car the chocolate bar is waiting just for you.

Jorja Jones (8)
Luckwell Primary School

LITTLE BUNNY RABBIT

Twitchy noses, sparkling eyes,
I love my bunny rabbit,
He was a lovely surprise.

Nibbling at a carrot,
Running on the grass,
See his eyes shining,
They look like polished glass.

Look how is fur blows in the wind,
Soft and fluffy just like cotton wool,
A little round tail looking like a ball.

He's got some floppy ears,
That hang down from his head,
He's also got some straw,
For his cosy bed.

My rabbit is my friend for life,
And that is very clear,
I love my rabbit dearly,
And I always will.

Amy Smith (8)
Luckwell Primary School

SPACE

Space is a place where it never ends.
It is dark, big and frightens me.
There are stars and the moon and other things too!
The comets are big, the planets are small
But the sun is the worst of them all.

Shauna Charles (8)
Luckwell Primary School

HOUSE OF HORRORS

Ever wondered what goes bump in the night?
Can't get asleep 'cause
You're shivering with fright
You never know
When it's going to strike
The sounds that go bump in the night

Ever wondered what goes bump in the night?
Like the dripping of a tap
The never-ending creaking of the door
The sound of a cry in the dark
You've never heard before
All the things that scare you tonight

Ever wondered what goes bump in the night?
Can't get asleep 'cause
You're shivering with fright
You never know
When it's going to strike
The sounds that go bump in the night

Rachel Moore (11)
Luckwell Primary School

SNAKES AND BIRDS

Snakes are brown and green.
Snakes are slithering all day long.
Snakes are flying from branch to branch.
Birds are fluttering all through the day.
Birds are chirping in the town.
Everybody is happy except for me.

Gemma Woodburn (8)
Luckwell Primary School

I'M A DOLPHIN

I weave around the sea all day,
Trying not to cry if I hurt myself.
My mum and dad are very cool.
I've got a girlfriend, her name is Amy.
We've got three children,
One named Jon, one named Paul and Lizzie.
We went to a park, a shark ate Lizzie.
But we got her back.
Then we went out for tea.
We had cod fish, prawns and crab.
We went back home to bed.
We had a fire in the night.
It was people dropping bombs.

Eloise Heybyrne (8)
Luckwell Primary School

MY PET SHARK

My pet shark smells like burnt sausage.
My pet shark eats everything.
My pet shark sleeps in sludge.
My pet shark loves to read books.
My pet shark always eats sweets.
My pet shark snores very, very loud.
My pet shark plays in sand all day.
My pet shark is asleep, please be quiet.

Sssshhh - zzzzzz

Michael Thomas (8)
Luckwell Primary School

FRIENDS

Get changed
Call for Kerry
'Are you coming out?'
'Yes.'
'Alright.'
'Hang on.'
'Where are we going?'
'Round mine if you want.'
'Alright.'
We play games
We play music
We watch TV
The best thing about it is
We get to chat
And I know I've got a friend

Kelly Anne Booth (11)
Luckwell Primary School

SNOW!

I opened my eyes and I jumped out of bed.
When I looked through the window I couldn't believe my eyes,
It was snowing!
It was exploding with snow.
The snow felt like ice cream
And when I stepped on it
It was crunchy.
I took my dog out.
He was catching snowballs.

Adam Beasmore (8)
Luckwell Primary School

BULLYING

Pinch, punch
Punch, pinch
Ouch!
That hurt
Don't bully
It hurts inside
Pinch, punch
Punch, pinch
Only because
I'm short
And you're tall
Don't bully
Pinch, punch
Punch, pinch
Stop that
I'm telling about you
You're a big tale tat tit
It still hurts inside.

Rachel Jones (10)
Luckwell Primary School

THE HORSE

The horse runs like the thunder shooting into the sky.
The horse carefully walks into breezy morning air.
The horse moves like a marathon runner.
The horse's eyes are like the deep blue of the ocean.
The horse's tail moves like the wavy wind.
The horse's breath explodes like a steaming kettle.

Frankie Marks (8)
Luckwell Primary School

PLANETS

The massive blazing sun is the hottest place,
Tiny Mars is known as the Red Planet,
Neptune is like a freezer.

The moon is full of big craters,
Pluto is a small purple planet,
Saturn is the multicoloured planet with loops.

Uranus, the light green planet,
Mercury, the hot grey planet,
Earth, the third planet from the sun.

Venus, the orange and yellow planet,
Jupiter, the biggest planet in our solar system,
The massive yellow sun is burning.

Martin Chamberlain (10)
Luckwell Primary School

THE ROBIN

Just as the glistening lantern peeps up from the grassy hills.
A black shadow falls across it.
The shadow of a beautiful small bird
Standing there silently.
It was a robin
Standing there with his big, glowing red disco light of a chest
Flashing with the wink of the sparkling sun
And his brown feathers like the wood on a burning fire.

Iona Baker (8)
Luckwell Primary School

Dolphin

Dolphins are playful
Dolphins are graceful
Dolphins are clever
They jump through the deep blue oceans
They glide through the crashing waves
They dive through the sea of silvery fish.

Charlotte Stoddart (8)
Luckwell Primary School

My Rat

My rat is very fat
He is all black and has a white belly
His paws are white too
He is cute and he doesn't bite
He is very smooth
His whiskers are very long, like fine sticks
He wiggles his little pink nose
He scrunches up his eyes.

Thomas Wilkox (8)
Luckwell Primary School

The Young Man

There was a young man from Bristol
Who wanted to buy a big pistol
He got into a fight
But his aim wasn't right
That daring young man from Bristol

Tim Jones (11)
Luckwell Primary School

The Snow

Down comes the snow
Children looking out the window
When it settles
Making snowmen everywhere
Children playing on their sledges
Parents chatting
Snowboards racing down the hill.

Luke Kibby (10)
Luckwell Primary School

A Snowman

A snowman is very cold,
A snowman is very bold,
A snowman is chalk white,
A snowman will never bite,
A snowman is made out of snow,
When a snowman melts he is very low!

Rory Notton (9)
Luckwell Primary School

Happy

Happy is bright yellow,
Happy smells like spring flowers,
Happy tastes like ice cream in the summer,
Happy sounds like children playing,
Happy feels soft and smooth,
Happy lives in your heart.

Danielle Upham (9)
Luckwell Primary School

MY HOLIDAY

Day by day
Week by week
The time
Just drags on
Three days
Two days
One day
Now time is almost done
We're in the car
Time's running fast
One hour thirty minutes
Fifteen minutes
And 10, 9, 8
Come on 7, 6, 5
Nearly 4, 3, 2
Yes!
Out of the car
I feel like I'm walking on air
Off we go to the beach
Just gran, gramps, Catherine, dad, mum and me.

Charlotte Daw (11)
Luckwell Primary School

THERE WAS A YOUNG MAN, NAME OF HOWARD

There was a young man, name of Howard
Whose brain was solar powered
When it was bright
He could do sums or write
But he just went to sleep when it showered

Dan Howard (11)
Luckwell Primary School

Is Santa As Normal As We Are?

Does Santa go to the galleries
To buy football boots?
Or does he stay in the North Pole
Or does he use razors?

Does Santa go to the supermarket
Just to 'pay here'?
Or does he play on Space Invaders
Or does he fly on his reindeer?

Does Santa get angry
And use words like 'Shove off'?
Or does he like everyone
Or does he play with Rudolph?

Does Santa have a haircut
Or does he wear a hat?
Personally I think he'd look good
With a Santa baseball cap!

Conner Glanville (9)
Luckwell Primary School

Anger

Anger is red and orange,
Anger smells like copper burning and melting,
Anger tastes like red-hot chilli peppers,
Anger sounds like scratching on a blackboard,
Anger feels like walking on a stony beach,
Anger lives inside your soul.

Thomas Reading (10)
Luckwell Primary School

GAMES

Games are entertainment
Games are the best
You play them in the playground
And use them for fun
There are lots of games
Like sports and logic
Computer games
And much, much more
You get them in the shop
Or make them up
Anyway you're sure
To have fun

Callum Herbert (10)
Luckwell Primary School

IF I WAS ANDY COLE

If I was Andy Cole
I would be great
The fans would sing
'Andy Cole, Andy Cole, Andy, Andy Cole.'
He kicks the ball and scores a goal
Andy, Andy Cole,
I'd kick the ball
And score a goal
And the fans
Would all go wild
If I was Andy Cole.

Blaine Carroll (11)
Luckwell Primary School

5, 4, 3, 2, 1, LIFT-OFF!

I flew to space and this is what I saw . . .

I saw the humongous burning sun,
I saw the sharp-edged stars.
I saw Jupiter, Saturn, Earth,
Pluto, Mercury and Mars.

The moon was rotten, quiet and scary,
I didn't like it at all.
I kept looking back at my massive shuttle,
I was careful not to fall.

I smelt a funny smell around me,
It smelt like rotten egg.
I got frozen and started,
To get goose pimples on my leg.

Alex Mallett (10)
Luckwell Primary School

ANIMALS

Tigers, tigers
Bears, bears
They're so cuddly
Under the stairs
Hamsters, hamsters
Cats and cats
They curl up
On your lap.

May Barnes (11)
Luckwell Primary School

PLANETS

I like the planet Mars,
I also like looking at stars,
Mars is not made of clay,
And nor is the Milky Way.

The surface is covered in dust,
And you know it's a must,
For us to visit soon,
As we did years ago with the moon.

There is talk of UFOs,
And it's gossip, as it goes,
When the first spaceman got out and ran,
He bumped into a little green man!

Chelsea Tanner (9)
Luckwell Primary School

CONCORDE

Like a white sonic swan
He flies above me
Like a dynamic swallow
He dives around me
Like a razor
He almost cuts me
Like a chimney
He chokes me
The giant of the sky.

Ryan Stuckes (10)
Luckwell Primary School

@ Bristol

@ Bristol is the best,
But when you come home you need a rest,
You can be a presenter,
Or a camera man,
Or even play volleyball,
It is so cool!

You can take a photo of your shadow,
I give @ Bristol a big *bravo!*
Even though it costs a lot,
It's worth every penny in the pot!
I didn't really want to come home,
It's even better than the *Millennium Dome!*

Laura Rhodes (10)
Luckwell Primary School

My New Scooter

I've got a new scooter
I like going down hills
It makes your eyes water
All you can hear is
Whoosh, whoosh
I go so fast
But I can't fall off
As it's really painful
But I love
Riding on my new scooter.

George Nelmes (10)
Luckwell Primary School

FOOTBALL

We are on the way to the League Cup Final
The manager will pick the team
The match is about to start
Our team is confident
To go out and win
We are going on the pitch
Our supporters cheer us on
1-0, 2-0, 3-0, 4-0, 4-1, 4-2, 4-3
I don't think we will win
It's gone to penalties
Oh! No!
Come on lads
We can beat them
The ball hits the post
The ball hits the bar
They get to have the last penalty
If they miss we'll win
The pressure is all on us
They've missed!
We've won!
Yeeaahh!
Come on, let's go to the bar
The manager shouts,
'The drinks are on me.'
The players sing,
'Say we are top of the League,'
'Say we are top of the League.'

Giorgio Mancini (10)
Luckwell Primary School

WALKING TO SCHOOL

This morning I walked to school,
This morning my good friend picked me up,
This morning I walked along the very wide road,
This morning I saw a big yellow car.

This morning I saw the lovely lollipop lady,
This morning I went past the small sweet shop,
This morning I walked on the green, green grass,
This morning I took my yummy packed lunch into the hall.

This morning I walked into the empty hall,
This morning I walked into the lovely classroom,
This morning I said hello to my lovely teacher!

Tayler Maggs (9)
Luckwell Primary School

MEG

Meg is a furry pup,
With softness all around,
Meg is a playful bouncy pup,
Who has a treat that is meat,
Meg is a furry pup,
That enjoys jumping around,
Meg's best mate is me,
I open the creaky gate for her,
Meg is a sporty pup who runs up hills,
And leaps around the place,
Meg sleeps in a basket with two soft blankets,
Meg is my best friend and I am hers.

Sophie Christopher (9)
Luckwell Primary School

PLANETS AND SPACE

The moon is like a shiny silver ball.
The sun is like a blazing fire.
The Earth is a spinning sphere.

Stars are shooting and zooming.
Rockets are landing and flying.
Meteors are crashing and bashing.

Jupiter is massive.
Saturn is distant.
Mars is hot and close as well.

Mercury is by Venus, a very happy place.
Venus is a lovely planet.
Neptune sounds like a sea.

Pluto is one of the smallest and the last place.
Uranus is a bumpy planet.
When the universe is gone everyone and thing are gone.

James Powell (9)
Luckwell Primary School

CYPRUS

Cyprus is a lovely country,
Cyprus is a very small place,
Cyprus is scorching,
Cyprus has a dazzling sun in the sky.
Cyprus is very extraordinary,
Cyprus is super,
Cyprus is excellent,
Cyprus is famous for its ice cream.

James Charles (9)
Luckwell Primary School

FAMILY

My mum . . .
Cute and sweet
She's quiet for a mum
She's the best mum ever

My dad . . .
The biggest in the family
He is the oldest
He is scary sometimes

Me . . .
I'm brilliant at football
I'm the smallest but I don't care
I'm the sportiest in my family

My sister . . .
My sister is the kindest
The sweetest
And the most perfect sister ever

Sam Skidmore (10)
Luckwell Primary School

THE MOON

The moon is big
The moon is small
The moon is happy
The moon is sad
The moon is cheese
The moon is green
And the moon has a face
That smiles at us.

Tom Hill (10)
Luckwell Primary School

OLD VIC NATIVITY PLAY

The Nativity was funny,
It could have had more laughter,
The three kings were shiny and clean,
That made them bad and mean.

The Nativity was funny,
It could have had more laughter,
The shepherds were old and rusty,
That made them poor and dusty.

The Nativity was funny,
It could have had more laughter,
The donkey was called Beckham,
Who met the baby sent from Heaven!

Ricky Barrett (9)
Luckwell Primary School

@ BRISTOL

We're going to @ Bristol to day,
Because there is lots of things to do and play,
@ Bristol is fun,
There's treats for you and everyone.

The Imaginarium is really cool,
It is so big, in it you could fit a swimming pool,
@ Bristol is the best,
It is so good that it has beaten all the rest!

Joe Care (9)
Luckwell Primary School

Party Food

Plates are rattling on the table,
Animal biscuits are tasty snacks,
Really yummy Coke in my plastic cup,
The chocolate fingers are really lovely,
Yummy chocolate rolls are scrumptious.

Finding delicious food to fill my tummy,
On the table were biscuits,
Open our mouths and sing happy birthday,
Day for celebration is the best thing of all.

Mathew Wherlock (9)
Luckwell Primary School

Planets

The dangerous red Jupiter,
Danger red loopter,
The massive sun is a big bun.

Saturn likes to draw patterns,
Mars bar on Mars.

The Earth is as smearth,
The smearth is a blue green Earth,
Mercury wants mercy!

Benito Mancini (9)
Luckwell Primary School

THE DARK DARK FOREST

As I walk through the dark, dark forest,
I see my old friend Boris,
He was making a white, cloth, ghost,
And I saw a piece of lovely, hot toast.
The forest is growing gloomy and dark,
I saw a piece of brown bark,
I slapped Boris on the back,
Then someone hit me back.
I quickly ran on home,
Then I heard a moan,
It was Casey,
Moaning at Stacey,
Boris woke me up,
And said it was all a dream,
He thought I was in the land of ice cream!

Rebecca Weaver (9)
Oldbury Court Primary School

THERE WAS A FIGHT IN THE NIGHT

There was a fight in the night
With a bear and a chair
The bear was hanging from the branch.
The chair was clapping for fun
But then it stopped, the bear roared.
The mud said it was dying
When it started to rain.
Suddenly the chair pinched the bear's finger
The bear sped off and the chair said yes.

Sam Fletcher (9)
Oldbury Court Primary School

THE DARKEST NIGHT OF THE YEAR

The wind blew hard and cruel.
The storm was coming like it should,
Because it was that time of year.
In buckets the rain came down
Soaking the rider as he sped through the night.
The dawn was getting closer
Like a lion waiting to pounce.
Slowly the light in the sky crept nearer,
Houses and trees began to appear
It felt like a bright new year.
The sun came up but nothing could stop his gallop,
The look on his face was . . . fright,
Like a lion the dawn got closer,
Like a lion waiting to pounce.

Elly Robbins (9)
Oldbury Court Primary School

THE FOREST OF MYSTERIES

There is a forest far, far away.
This forest is harmless by day -
But by night it is murderous!

Few people go in and none ever come out - alive!
Foul phantoms frighten even the fiercest foreigners
Who dare to enter their lair.

People say that some day there deadly demons
Will somehow disappear.
But the wood will still be feared by everyone.

Eliot Glasspole (9)
Oldbury Court Primary School

THE MYSTERY

The waves are crashing,
It's very smashing
It's dark at night,
The street lights are bright,
The moon goes boom,
A witch flies up high,
Into the mysterious sky,
On the gold moon lays her broom,
You can look and stare but
No one knows she's there.
She flies down,
With her broom,
She goes into her room
A ghost is sat on the bed,
I hear a scream,
A girl is sat in a chair,
Her hair is like a polar bear,
The witch is there with a spoon
She does it in the moonlight moon,
I hear a scream
Ahhhhhhhhhh!

Courtenay Grey (9)
Oldbury Court Primary School

FEAR

It was a dark and gloomy night.
The wind howled in the night.
Wilder and wilder!
A rustle in the bush,
A crackle under my foot,
A hiss behind my shoulder.
Fear tingles up my spine.
It might be a monster,
It might be a rat,
No . . . it's a soft pussy cat,
I need not be afraid!

Jade Phillips (8)
Oldbury Court Primary School

THE DARK, DARK WOOD

I walked through the dark, dark wood,
Pushing the leaves outside.
I suddenly froze and looked,
I saw something black
I looked up and saw a crowd of bats
I turned and shouted *help!*

I started to run and scream,
The bats started chasing me,
I ran as fast as I could,
I got home just in time.

Levi Mapstone (9)
Oldbury Court Primary School

Mystery Dream

I go to turn my light off,
And fall into a deep sleep.
I'm in a dark forest,
I hear howling and rattling.
Suddenly a train comes through my door,
I get on the train, it's a mystery train,
It takes me through the scary forest.
I see wolves howling,
Bats flying,
And a flickering shadow.
I wake up
The shadow is still there!
Was it really just my lava lamp?

Sophie Jane Brine (9)
Oldbury Court Primary School

Through The Countryside

Faster than lightning louder than rattles
Rainbows and rivers, campers and cattle
Faster than raindrops bigger than forests
Foxes and ditches, hedges and pitches
Slower than grandma, colder that snow
Postman and papers people and places
Slower than traffic smaller than buses
Dutches and ditches, people and suitcases
Swifter than raindrops hotter than the sun
People and postbox, children and rooftops.

Ceejay Dun (9) & Alex West (10)
Shirehampton Primary School

MEMORIES

Memories are special you will never forget
You might have been at the seaside getting wet
It might have been a present or a sunny holiday
Or it could have been a dream while in your bed you lay
You will always treasure your memories no matter what
And all the good times that have passed will never be forgot.

Amberley Gazzard (10)
Shirehampton Primary School

THE SLEEPOVER

The girls arrived for the sleepover tonight
It wasn't long before the first pillow fight.
Chocolate and crisps eaten all night.
We all saw a spider and jumped in a fright.

Charlotte Allan (10) & Dannielle Harris (10)
Shirehampton Primary School

CITIES AND COUNTRYSIDES

Faster than lightning, louder than rattles
Rainbows and rivers, campers and cattle.
Swifter than raindrops, smaller than towers
Children and cities, police cars and power
Slower than grandma, hotter than cookers
Stations and skateboards, boats and bookers.

Christopher James Higgs (8)
Shirehampton Primary School

CATS

Twas the middle of the night
There was nothing in sight
Everyone was a slumber
Except Pouchy and Gumper

They were chasing wee rats
Till they got to their mats
Together running around
Till they fell to the ground

Pouncing all the way home
Across the rooftops past the garden gnome
Through the cat flap
And had a nice nap

Amy Hembrough & Jordhanna Hudson (10)
Shirehampton Primary School

FASTER THAN

Faster than hedgehogs, faster than robbers,
Rainbows and rivers, tree trunks and tractors
Louder than children, louder than lorries
Postmen and people, places and robbers.
Slower than snowflakes, slower than shotguns,
People and trolleys, taxis and coaches
Louder than Woolworth's, louder than classrooms.

Jessica Lenagh (8)
Shirehampton Primary School

NONSENSE POEM

I wake up in the morning
I wake up in the morning and get out of my bath
I wake up in the morning and have a bed
I wake up in the morning and eat my teeth
I wake up in the morning and clean my breakfast
I wake up in the morning and come down the door
I wake up in the morning and put my seat on me
I wake up in the morning and I sit on my bag
I wake up in the morning and go out the stairs

Kelsey Cox (9) & Kimberley Sheppard (10)
Shirehampton Primary School

FUNNY FACES

Funny faces
Fat and thin
Have you put the eyebrows in?
Maybe they're the size of a pin.

Sparkling eyes
Tells lies
Some eyes are blue which makes you frown
Watch out if they are brown.

Luke Daniel Krupa (10)
Shirehampton Primary School

FASTER THAN

Faster than lightning,
Louder than thunder
Woolworth's and Co-op,
Pet shops and Argos
Slower than grandma,
Colder than snowflakes
Postman and postbox
Robbers and rooftops.

Amy Richardson (9)
Shirehampton Primary School

MY DOG SPOT

I have a white dog
Whose name is Spot,
And he's sometimes white
And he's sometimes not.
But whether he's white
Or whether he's not,
There's a patch on his ear
That makes him Spot.

He has a tongue
That is long and pink,
And he rolls it out
When he wants to think,
He seems to think most
When the weather is hot.
He is a wise sort of dog,
Is my dog Spot.

Teresa Licata (9)
SS Peter & Paul RC Primary School

THE SNAKE

My name's Jake,
As you know I'm a snake
Don't mess with me,
My poison's not fake.

Green and black is my colour
My eyes are like fire,
Don't sing sweet music,
Don't play me the liar.

In the ground where I live
There is nothing much to do,
I wish I was up there,
Then I could bite you!

Davide Lattuca (9)
SS Peter & Paul RC Primary School

DRAGON

A fat fierce dragon who stamps everywhere
Who breathes flaming fire a very
Angry looming creature moves as everyday
Moves with spikes, sharp claws and blood
Thirsty dragon he smells like fish he has
Blood dripping down his teeth a four foot
Dragon a two horned dragon
He had a horse's body
And a dragon's head.

Daniella Ruffino (8)
SS Peter & Paul RC Primary School

Is There A Place For Me?

This is my life not full of glee,
The question is, is it for me?
I'm carrying on with my life
Not taking a break or making strife.

My greatest idol is the great glimmering ocean of mystery and awe,
I've never wanted to stay somewhere so much before,
The sea has power, the sea is mysterious but most of all the sea has a
place.

I see the cliffs there, rough and great and in no fury,
They make you praise them in the glory,
The cliffs are rough, the cliffs are great, but most of all the cliffs have
a place.

The sea has a place,
The cliffs have a place,
And now I've found my place.

Simon White (10)
SS Peter & Paul RC Primary School

Shells

Each seashell is intricately designed
The grooves like roads, all combined.
All the sandy shells, sitting on the beach,
Waiting for the shell collectors, waiting to be reached.
All the seashells not ashore,
All laid on the ocean floor.

Tom Wright (11)
SS Peter & Paul RC Primary School

THE SEAGULL'S JOURNEY

I flapped my white wings
Pushing thin air to the side,
And rose up in the snowy clouds
I looked below, many things I saw.

Below me was grainy, yellow sand,
I could see people playing, swimming smoothly, calmly,
Other seagulls resting on the jagged rocks, sticking
Out of the sheer, abrupt cliff like pins in someone's
Thumb. This is my home.

Rolling fields. Cows grazing, lying down on thin blades
Of grass. Flocks of sheep resting like a fluffy cloud
Upon the sky. A cool breeze makes the long grass
Wave peacefully. I fly through a cloud, the country is gone.

Car engines roar as if they're trying to scare other vehicles.
Skyscrapers touch the sky, scraping the clouds.
Children yelling, people skateboarding
Fumes surround the would-be-fresh-air. Pollution reigns here.

The city, the country, the sea is my home.

Johnny Creamer (11)
SS Peter & Paul RC Primary School

ON THE SEASHORE

On the sandy seashore sit in the scorching sun,
Watch the small children having fun.
Walk over to the craggy rockpools,
See pinching crabs and tiny shrimps
Or if you're brave and adventurous
Climb the colossal cliffs.

Sophie O'Kelly (10)
SS Peter & Paul RC Primary School

Sea Horizon

The shore is made of lots of sand,
Aesthetic, radiant, gleaming land,
A sparkling, warm, sandy cove,
Sunny and subtropical like a red-hot stove.

Splish splash, dash dash,
The waves ripple to beyond the horizon.

The water shallow and rather cold,
The cliffs black, damp and old,
An octopus waves its many legs,
A crab's pincers are like spiky clothes pegs.

Splish splash, dash dash,
The waves ripple to beyond the horizon.

The place is deserted, next to the sea,
As calm, bright and pretty as can be,
The only sounds heard are the arrival of waves
And gurgling from sunless sea caves.

Splish splash, dash dash,
The waves ripple to beyond the horizon.

Spitter, spatter.

David McCalley (10)
SS Peter & Paul RC Primary School

The Mouse

I climb up the stairs
I creep around the floor
I climb around the kitchen
I creep around the door!

I nibble on apples,
I nibble at an orange
I eat grapes
I slurp down porridge!

Kei Bergh (10)
SS Peter & Paul RC Primary School

DARKNESS

Darkness, darkness,
Big and black.
Darkness, darkness,
Sometimes not.

Darkness, darkness,
With a big white moon,
Darkness, darkness,
Looming over me.

Darkness, darkness,
Over the sea,
Darkness, darkness,
Do you have any friends?

Darkness, darkness,
I hate you!
Darkness, darkness,
Very naughty.

Darkness, darkness,
Come out of your lair,
Darkness, darkness, darkness, darkness,
I'm not afraid of you!

Lauren Cherry (8)
SS Peter & Paul RC Primary School

CHANGES

Changes happen all the time,
Like the seasons and the weather,
Even birds change,
From dull to stunning feathers.

Some people like changes,
Some people don't and get upset,
Some people cry because they're sad,
Maybe also because the changes are very bad.

The sky changes from grey to blue,
The sea changes from turquoise to green,
The country changes from bare to colour,
Letting the person in charge take over,
Mother Nature.

I can like changes,
But also hate them,
I like to change things around at home,
Especially in my bedroom.

If only people realised changes happen,
And take them more seriously
Many people don't,
So please God,
Help me!

Louise Marie Celine Walker (10)
SS Peter & Paul RC Primary School

DRAGON

The dragon with a smelly belly
Loves to kill and will
Hates light loves to fight
Teeth like knives loves to kill lives.

Claws like pins with slimy skin
Destroys everything in its path, cracks it in half
The dragon with a fiery breath, loves to lie and fly
He is very strong but does so much wrong.

Callum Craig (9)
SS Peter & Paul RC Primary School

WHEN I AM ALONE AT HOME

I once was at home
On my own in bed
But I didn't think I was alone
And when I go to school I think
Someone is coming with me
It might be a ghost
Because he sticks his
Magic trick on me
Everybody sticks at me
Then I faint and say
I am creepy
Then I wake up
Slowly I sing
No one is there
Then I see a creepy sign
Saying
'Welcome to Creep Town'
Children going to school
Happily they run
I suddenly woke up
It was only a dream.

Jakita Anderson (8)
SS Peter & Paul RC Primary School

DARKNESS

The dreaded darkness
Covers the clouds and the sun.
The looming darkness
Wraps around the house.

It comes to fight
The light.
The wicked darkness
Feels happy.

The evil darkness
Crawls over the village
The dreaded darkness
Feels sad when the
Light comes out.

Simone Price (8)
SS Peter & Paul RC Primary School

DRAGON

There was a grim fiery dragon,
He was a scary fierce one,
What happened to him was a legend,
But I know for certain he had,
Mean sharp claws, claws just like a normal dragon,
His tail is spiky and muscley, he drags it along the floor.
He makes a big roaring bellow,
You can tell he is quite sure.
And we said he was a legend,
And for all and all and you
Again he was a legend
For me and you both knew.

Sean Rice (9)
SS Peter & Paul RC Primary School

DARKNESS

I am the night
The pitch-black night
I am dark and I am scary
I give people frights.

I am the night
The big huge night
I cover the whole world
With a big white moon.
And the skies little stars
They twinkle, they twinkle
And are very bright
But I will always be as black
As the huge, black night.

Mahanagh Adams (8)
SS Peter & Paul RC Primary School

ON THE PIER

On the creaky wooden pier I walk along
Jumping over the gaps looking down into
The deep blue sea.
The powerful waves lap over each other
Splashing clear water high into the air,
As the glistening sun beats down on me.

The wind blows gently in the air cooling
People down, and smiling children lick
Ice creams greedily.
The boiling sun starts to set, as everyone
Leaves the creaky wooden pier and now
I'm left standing here all alone.

Phoebe Farrell (11)
SS Peter & Paul RC Primary School

CHRISTMAS

It was the night before Christmas in that little old house,
Not a single thing was moving, not even a mouse.
All the children were sleeping in their cosy beds,
Dreaming about the next day was what was happening in their heads.

When the clock struck twelve on that cold and wet night,
Someone came down the chimney 'Who's that?'
The children said with fright.
It was jolly good Santa Claus with his sack full of toys,
All for the young Christmas joys.

The next morning the children woke with glee,
And ran downstairs singing Christmas carols happily.
When they saw the presents under the tree they said,
'I hope some of those are for me.'

When their parents came down to find them awake,
They said 'What are you doing up at this time for goodness sake?'
The reply came from a young girl called Louise,
'Can we open our presents Mammy? Oh please! Please!'

Mammy looked around, sighed and said,
'Well okay, but just wait for grandma to get out of bed.'
When grandma stepped into the room the children rushed to the tree,
And started to open their presents joyfully.

At nine o'clock the children went up to bed,
Then went to sleep with a story, which grandma read.

Cian O'Carroll-Lolait (11)
SS Peter & Paul RC Primary School

I Somehow Discovered

I somehow discovered a nit
Right at the bottom of a pit
I picked him up and put him in a cup
That's how I discovered a nit.

I somehow discovered a shoe
I saw it get flushed down the loo,
I went down to get it
I only just missed it
That's how I discovered a shoe.

I somehow discovered a mouse
I found him in my house,
He looked stupidly small,
But then *gloriously* tall
That's how I discovered a mouse.

I somehow discovered a bed
Right on top of my head
I got a headache
Then a tummy ache
That's how I discovered my bed.

I somehow discovered a witch
Standing in the middle of a football pitch,
She was *enormously* fat
With a pointed hat
That's how I discovered a witch.

Kasia Everett (8)
SS Peter & Paul RC Primary School

MY FRIENDS

My name is Carrie Collins
I'm going to tell you about my friends,
I don't know why I care so much
Because they drive me round the bend.

The first friend I'm going to tell you about
Her name is Sophie Mast,
She's very nice and kind to me
She's the best girl in our class.

I can't forget Mary Stevens
She's the cleverest of them all,
Everything's easy to Mary
She's the know-it-all.

My best friend is Natalie Seymore
My second is Allison Tree,
But they're not the only ones I like
They act like they're family.

Roisin Walsh (10)
SS Peter & Paul RC Primary School

AUTUMN

A   pples are growing on the trees to be picked,
U   clean leaves eventually fall
T   urkey for us to eat,
U   nlike today, leaves are falling and hitting the ground
M   arrows grow in the fields
N   ice shaped leaves start to fall.

Anthony Brandrick (10)
SS Peter & Paul RC Primary School

HIGH UP IN THE SKY

As tall as the clouds themselves hanging over like leading towers
                                                                up in heaven.
Bricks falling down towards the calm dusty ground.

Seagulls flying high up into the sky ducking and dodging
Around the crumbling bricks.

Me standing on top of cliffs, my belly rumbling like bees in a hive
It gives me a nerve to walk to the edge.

Almost like I was threatening myself to fall off the crumbling rocky
                                                                grey cliffs
My heart is pounding for me not to do it but I am sorry
I have a nerve just to do it.

Tyrone Shaw (10)
SS Peter & Paul RC Primary School

DRAGON, DRAGON

Dragon, dragon big and tall
Dragon, dragon blood and bones
Dragon, dragon smells of rotten fish
Dragon, dragon takes people away
Dragon, dragon yellow and green
Dragon, dragon he smells of fire
Dragon, dragon eyeballs coming out
Dragon, dragon spits out fire
Dragon, dragon throws people away
Dragon, dragon see those bones.

Cecile Jones (9)
SS Peter & Paul RC Primary School

THE SEA OF DREAMS

The sea slowly drifts along the shore
There is no noise anymore
The seagulls fly extremely high
Soaring through the deep blue sky.

The sand is golden brown
Like golden dust on a crown
The sand queen makes her way
Through the yellow sandy lane
She comes here nearly every day.

The enchanting fish
Swim through the green weeds
Hitting the gentle floor
Their scales glittering like beads

Aishu Subramanyain (11)
SS Peter & Paul RC Primary School

STARS

When I sit and watch
The stars it makes
Me think a lot about Mars
The shiny silver stars
Shining down, spying on the ground.
The starlight is like a huge spotlight.
I wonder what it's like to touch one,
That's a dream come true
But until that day I'll sit and wonder!

Phoebe Potter (10)
SS Peter & Paul RC Primary School

MONSTERS

My mother told me to go to bed
But I didn't dare
Because I knew there was a
Monster waiting on the stairs.

I ran into the kitchen
And banged my head on the sink
My dad said 'Watch it in there'
My nose was very pink

I ran into the cellar
And smashed into Dad's best wine
A ghost appeared from nowhere
And said 'Go away you swine.'

Jamie Connett (9)
SS Peter & Paul RC Primary School

THE FARM

On the farm lay the sheep
All warm in the straw asleep
Every spring there's a different foal
Each one with a different soul
We have two sheep dogs,
Who chase away the frogs
On the farm there's a pony
Called Midge he's very, very
Nice except he's scared of
Crossing the bridge.

Emily Poole (9)
SS Peter & Paul RC Primary School

DARK SPACE

I have been to space and it is very dark
So be calm in space for it is very dark
You have got to have a lot of guts to go in space
So be careful because you might meet your fate
You just might crash the ship
For you are quite thick

Angelo Amato (10)
SS Peter & Paul RC Primary School

CATS!

Some cats are wild, some cats are tame,
Some cats like cream in their milk or some like it plain.
Some cats like biscuits, and some like their meat.
Some cats fight with every other cat they meet.
Cats here, cats there,
Cats are nearly
Everywhere!

Amelia Scanlan (7)
SS Peter & Paul RC Primary School

FOOTBALL

Football, football is my game
Football, football suits my name
Football, football is really cool
Football, football's fab at school
Football, football is the best
Football's better than all the rest.

Remi Bergh (8)
SS Peter & Paul RC Primary School

WINTER

Flimsy snowflakes gently fall
Gathered up to make a ball
Children build a man of snow
Happy faces all aglow
The world is blanketed with white
Bright against the dark of night.

The leaves are gone, the trees are bare
Is there any life out there?
There's robin with red breast
Carrying twigs to build a nest
Cats and dogs shiver and hide
Dreaming of the fireside.

Christmas is here at long last
With happy times which go too fast
Presents, parcels, cards and gifts
Let's hope Santa's read his list
I wish winter was always here
And Christmas was three times a year!

Katie Creamer (9)
SS Peter & Paul RC Primary School

DRAGON

A dragon who hates light but loves to fight
A dragon who never can sleep but loves eating sheep
A dragon with silky skin and claws as sharp as a pin
A dragon with teeth like knives that loves to kill lives
A dragon with legs so strong and wings so long.

Sean O'Kelly (8)
SS Peter & Paul RC Primary School

DRAGON

Dragon, dragon with fiery breath
Dragon, dragon with a heart full of theft.

Dragon, dragon with skin like a hide
Dragon, dragon you have never cried.

Dragon, dragon we know you're large
Dragon, dragon we will still charge.

Dragon, dragon as we clash
Dragon, dragon you will thrash.

Dragon, dragon with blood so black
Dragon, dragon with no love to crack.

Dragon, dragon with only one eye
Dragon, dragon I don't want to die.

Dragon, dragon as you have no heart
Dragon, dragon you will fall apart.

William Foster-Grundy (9)
SS Peter & Paul RC Primary School

DARKNESS

The darkness looms all over the town
As its hand comes crushing down
He covers the place with his big face
He's like a giant with a mace
But don't be scared for he's alright
He wants to (he wants to) play and not fight
So next time you're out at night
Please please don't have a fright.

Perran Mitchell (8)
SS Peter & Paul RC Primary School

THERE WAS A MAN-EATING EAGLE

There was once a man-eating eagle,
Who suddenly ate a seagull,
He felt quite funny
With a bird in his tummy
And the next day he found it was illegal.

Hannah Giebus (8)
SS Peter & Paul RC Primary School

DARKNESS

The darkness goes down and all around
When the darkness covers the moon the owls hoot.
At night the dreaded darkness
Crawls over the village
The wicked darkness walks all over you.
The darkness said 'I give you a fright
I have no family, I'm not that happy.
Don't be scared I will wrap you in my bed
I'll twirl you around and make you safe and sound.'

Hope Alkins (8)
SS Peter & Paul RC Primary School

THERE WAS AN OLD MAN OF WAR

There was an old man of war
Who was a terrible bore
He sat on a stone
And made me moan
Then he went back to war.

Claudia Gocoul (7)
SS Peter & Paul RC Primary School

WHY ARE YOU LATE FOR SCHOOL?

I didn't get up
Because I was too tired,
And I was too tired
Because I went to bed late
And I went to bed late
Because I watched TV till the middle of the night
And I watched TV till the middle of the night
Because my mum said I could
Because I was good
And I was good
Because I wanted to be good
I am late sir
Because I wanted to be good.

Lydia Kellett (7)
SS Peter & Paul RC Primary School

HAIR

Hair is blonde, hair is black
It is weaving down your back.

Hair is ginger, hair is brown
Sometimes it is tumbling down.

Hair is curly, hair is straight
Put it up when you're going out on a date.

Hair is yours, hair is mine,
We'll have it for all time.

Eleanor King (8)
SS Peter & Paul RC Primary School

ANIMAL POEM

A dog called Ben
Got up one day
Barking at Betty
Rolling in the hay

Now Betty a black and white horse
Liked nothing better than to run the course
She galloped across the field and sat
And was welcomed by Fitz the cat.

Fitz purred and ran and then stops
To watch snowy the rabbit
Who runs then hops.

A dog barks
A horse gallops
A cat purrs
A rabbit hops.

Animals *can* be friends!

Connie Short (9)
The Tynings School

JESUS MY FRIEND

Jesus can do anything
Jesus is the mighty king
He carries me when I am low
And walks beside me as I grow
He's the friend who looks after me
He shows me everything I see.

Kate-Louise Fry (8)
The Tynings School

My Brother

He does not let me play his game
I always get the blame
It is a shame
His teeth are dirty yellow
He always wants to bellow
He always wants to fight
He wakes up in the night
Because he gets a fright
He always looks a sight
He likes to boast
And puts jam on his toast
He likes to play with guns
And eat creamy buns
He always gets shouted at by my mother
He is my brother.

Claudia Jacob (8)
The Tynings School

Animal Poem

Cats and rats are very cute
    Dogs and frogs make funny noises
        Seahorses and horses are very clever
        Eels and seals like swimming
          Lice and mice and creepy
            Foxes and cocks
              Eagles and beagles
                  Zorillas and gorillas
          Dinos and rhinos are very smelly
            And hippos too!

Faye Anastasia Mason (9)
The Tynings School

STARTING FROM A SNAIL

Once there was a snail,
A very small snail,
He sat on a log,
A very small log.

On the log he met a mouse,
A very small mouse,
And the snail and the mouse went fishing!

In the pond they met a frog,
But the frog was quite big.
So they went to the forest,
But there wasn't much space,
So they went back to the pond.

And so the snail is now a water snail,
And the mouse is now a water rat
But the frog just stays as a frog.

Jack Andrews (9)
The Tynings School

PENNY POT

Penny Pot, Penny Pot I've got some money,
Money, money for your tummy.
If you've got some money,
Then put it in my tummy.
1p's, 2p's, doesn't matter what,
Just come along to put it in my pot.
10p's, 20p's and 5p's too.
My tummy's relying on you.
50p's £1's, come along today,
But please don't delay.

Samantha Wood (8)
The Tynings School

MY CAT JACK

I have a cat
His name is Jack
He falls asleep on the kitchen mat.

His fur is black and white
And he always goes out at night
He uses his cat flap to go in and out
But when it's raining you never see him out.

He always sits on my mummy's lap
He's such a cuddly cat
I love my pet Jack.

Jordan Powell (8)
The Tynings School

MY PETS

I have a cat called Tat, who has a shaped mat like a rat.
She has a bat that's a toy and she thinks it is a boy.
She has some little kittens, that have some little mittens.

I have a dog, whose name is Mog, he chases my frog around the garden.
Mog jogs in the fog, jumps over the log and lands on my little frog.
Frog leapt up and hit my cup, which landed on my poor little pup.

I have a bunny called Hunny, who looks a bit funny, I feed him loads of honey.
He costs me loads of money, it's been rather sunny
And my nose has been getting runny, but I think Hunny is rather funny.

Sophie Graham (8)
The Tynings School